THE EASY DASH DIET COOKBOOK FOR LAZY PEOPLE

1500 Days of Nutritious, Easy-to-Prepare Recipes to Maintain a Balanced,
Straightforward, and Delicious Diet, No Matter Your Schedule

Kimberly Alvarado

© Copyright 2024 by Kimberly Alvarado - **All rights reserved.**

The following book is provided below with the aim of delivering information that is as precise and dependable as possible. However, purchasing this book implies an acknowledgment that both the publisher and the author are not experts in the discussed topics, and any recommendations or suggestions contained herein are solely for entertainment purposes. It is advised that professionals be consulted as needed before acting on any endorsed actions.

This statement is considered fair and valid by both the American Bar Association and the Committee of Publishers Association, and it holds legal binding throughout the United States.

Moreover, any transmission, duplication, or reproduction of this work, including specific information, will be deemed an illegal act, regardless of whether it is done electronically or in print. This includes creating secondary or tertiary copies of the work or recorded copies, which are only allowed with the express written consent from the Publisher. All additional rights are reserved.

The information in the following pages is generally considered to be a truthful and accurate account of facts. As such, any negligence, use, or misuse of the information by the reader will result in actions falling solely under their responsibility. There are no scenarios in which the publisher or the original author can be held liable for any difficulties or damages that may occur after undertaking the information described herein.

Additionally, the information in the following pages is intended solely for informational purposes and should be considered as such. As fitting its nature, it is presented without assurance regarding its prolonged validity or interim quality. Mention of trademarks is done without written consent and should not be construed as an endorsement from the trademark holder.

TABLE OF CONTENTS

Chapter 1: Understanding the DASH Diet ... 11
- 1. What is the DASH Diet? ... 12
- 2. Key Principles of the DASH Diet ... 13
- 3. Getting Started ... 14

Chapter 2: Essential Alimentary Tips ... 17
- 1. Smart Shopping for the DASH Diet ... 18
- 2. Meal Prep Made Easy ... 19
- 3. Reading Food Labels ... 20

Chapter 3: Managing Sodium Intake ... 23
- 1. Why Sodium Matters ... 24
- 2. Low-Sodium Cooking Techniques ... 25
- 3. Dining Out on the DASH Diet ... 26

Chapter 4: Balancing Macronutrients ... 29
- 1. Understanding Macronutrients ... 30
- 2. Healthy Carbohydrates ... 31
- 3. Proteins and Fats ... 32

Chapter 5: Complementary Healthy Habits ... 35
- 1. Hydration and Its Importance ... 36
- 2. Stress Management Techniques ... 37
- 3. Sleep and Recovery ... 38

Chapter 6: Breakfast Recipes ... 41

1. Quick and Easy Breakfasts ... 41
- Classic Berry Almond Overnight Oats ... 41
- Peanut Butter Banana Overnight Oats ... 42
- Tropical Coconut Overnight Oats ... 42
- Berry Almond Sunrise Bowl ... 42
- Green Tropical Energy Bowl ... 43
- Peanut Butter Banana Bliss Bowl ... 43
- Cinnamon Spice Whole Grain Pancakes ... 44
- Blueberry Lemon Whole Grain Pancakes ... 44
- Apple Cinnamon Oatmeal Pancakes ... 45

2. Hearty and Savory Options ... 45
- Spinach and Mushroom Frittata ... 45
- Bell Pepper and Potato Frittata ... 46
- Asparagus and Goat Cheese Frittata ... 46
- Spicy Avocado Toast with Egg ... 47
- Mediterranean Avocado Toast ... 47
- Smoked Salmon Avocado Toast ... 47

Sunrise Berry & Granola Greek Yogurt Parfait 48
Tropical Coconut Greek Yogurt Parfait 48
Pomegranate and Pistachio Greek Yogurt Parfait 48

3. Breakfasts on the Go 49

Spinach and Feta Breakfast Burritos 49
Turkey and Avocado Ranch Burritos 49
Mushroom and Bell Pepper Breakfast Burritos 50
Spinach and Feta Muffin Tin Omelets 50
Mushroom and Swiss Muffin Tin Omelets 51
Turkey and Spinach Muffin Tin Omelets 51
Chia and Pumpkin Seed Power Bars 51
Almond Coconut Energy Bars 52
Pistachio and Date Breakfast Bars 52

CHAPTER 7: LUNCH RECIPES 55

1. Fresh and Light Salads 55

Mediterranean Chickpea Salad with Sun-Dried Tomatoes 55
Avocado and Chickpea Salad with Pomegranate 56
Greek Chickpea Salad with Herbed Yogurt Dressing 56
Citrus Kissed Quinoa and Black Bean Salad 57
Mediterranean Quinoa and Black Bean Salad 57
Tropical Quinoa and Black Bean Salad 58
Tropical Spinach and Strawberry Salad 58
Citrus Infused Spinach and Strawberry Salad 59
Spicy Spinach and Strawberry Salad with Poppy Seed Dressing 59

2. Hearty and Satisfying Sandwiches 60

Classic Grilled Chicken Wraps 60
Mediterranean Grilled Chicken Wraps 60
Spicy Thai Chicken Wraps 61
Classic Turkey and Avocado Sandwich 61
Mediterranean Turkey Wrap 61
Avocado Turkey Club Sandwich 62
Mediterranean Veggie Hummus Pita 62
Spicy Avocado Hummus Pita 63
Roasted Bell Pepper and Hummus Pita 63

3. Warm and Comforting Soups 63

Smoky Lentil and Spinach Soup 63
Moroccan Lentil and Veggie Stew 64
Italian Lentil and Tomato Soup 64
Creamy Tomato Basil Soup with Greek Yogurt 65
Smoky Roasted Tomato Soup 65
Spicy Tomato and Red Lentil Soup 66
Chicken and Wild Rice Soup with Mushrooms 66
Lemon Herb Chicken and Wild Rice Soup 67
Creamy Wild Rice and Mushroom Chicken Soup 68

CHAPTER 8: DINNER RECIPES 69

1. Simple and Delicious Entrées 69

- Herbed Citrus Salmon with Fennel 69
- Maple-Glazed Salmon with Sage 70
- Pistachio Crusted Salmon 70
- Mediterranean Grilled Chicken and Veggie Kabobs 70
- Lemon Herb Grilled Chicken with Asparagus 71
- Spicy Grilled Chicken with Bell Pepper Salsa 71
- Mediterranean Quinoa Stuffed Bell Peppers 72
- Quinoa & Turkey Stuffed Bell Peppers 72
- Cauliflower Rice and Bean Stuffed Peppers 73

2. One-Pot Wonders 73

- Mediterranean Quinoa and Roasted Vegetable Pilaf 73
- Curried Coconut Quinoa with Lentils 74
- Garlic Mushroom and Spinach Quinoa 75
- Sundried Tomato and Garlic Chicken Stew 75
- Coconut Curry Chicken Stew 75
- Mushroom and Barley Chicken Stew 76
- Mediterranean Bliss Baked Cod 76
- Spiced Orange Cod Delight 77
- Herb-Infused Cod and Asparagus 77

3. Pasta and Grain Dishes 78

- Whole Wheat Pasta Primavera with Spring Vegetables 78
- Creamy Avocado Whole Wheat Pasta 78
- Mediterranean Whole Wheat Pasta Toss 79
- Classic Barley and Mushroom Risotto 79
- Barley Risotto with Asparagus and Lemon 80
- Mushroom and Spinach Barley Risotto 80
- Ginger-Sesame Brown Rice with Edamame 81
- Coconut-Lime Brown Rice with Cashews 81
- Spicy Tomato Basil Brown Rice 82

CHAPTER 9: SNACK AND APPETIZER RECIPES 83

1. Healthy Snacks 83

- Spiced Maple Cinnamon Nut Mix 83
- Sesame Seed & Chia Energy Bites 84
- Pistachio & Cranberry Salt-free Trail Mix 84
- Apple Slices with Almond-Cinnamon Butter 84
- Banana Medallions with Peanut Butter and Flaxseeds 85
- Pear Wedges with Cashew Vanilla Spread 85
- Classic Carrot and Cucumber Sticks with Spiced Hummus 85
- Zesty Bell Pepper Sticks with Avocado Lime Hummus 86
- Snap Pea Crisps with Curry Yogurt Dip 86

2. Appetizers for Entertaining 86

- Herbed Goat Cheese Stuffed Cherry Tomatoes 86
- Mediterranean Tuna Stuffed Cherry Tomatoes 87
- Cucumber Feta Stuffed Cherry Tomatoes 87
- Creamy Spinach and Artichoke Dip 88

Zesty Lime Spinach Artichoke Dip..88
Mediterranean Spinach and Artichoke Hummus Dip...89
Mini Caprese Skewers...89
Smoked Salmon Caprese Bites...89
Pesto-Stuffed Cherry Tomatoes..90

3. Quick Bites...90

Zesty Lemon Herb Greek Yogurt Dip..90
Spicy Roasted Red Pepper and Yogurt Dip...91
Cucumber Mint Greek Yogurt Dip..91
Tropical Cottage Cheese Delight..91
Pineapple Cottage Cheese Salsa...92
Cottage Cheese Pineapple Rings..92
Honey Cinnamon Roasted Chickpeas..92
Garlic Parmesan Roasted Chickpeas..93
Spicy Turmeric Roasted Chickpeas..93

CHAPTER 10: DESSERTS AND TREATS..95

1. Fruit-Based Desserts..95

Cinnamon Spice Baked Apples..95
Maple Ginger Baked Apples...96
Almond Crunch Baked Apples..96
Mixed Berry and Chia Parfait..96
Pomegranate Pistachio Greek Yogurt Parfait..97
Kiwi Lime Greek Yogurt Parfait..97
Grilled Peaches with Honey and Thyme...98
Grilled Peach and Ricotta Crostini..98
Peaches Grilled with Vanilla and Ginger..98

2. Low-Sodium Sweet Treats...99

Cherry Pistachio Dark Chocolate Bark..99
Minty Orange Peel Dark Chocolate Bark..99
Rosemary Hazelnut Dark Chocolate Bark...100
Classic Low-Sodium Oatmeal Raisin Cookies...100
Almond Oatmeal Cookies with Date Purée...101
Oatmeal Spice Cookies...101
Classic Vanilla Chia Seed Pudding..102
Chocolate Hazelnut Chia Pudding...102
Peanut Butter and Jelly Chia Pudding...102

3. Refreshing Beverages...103

Lavender Lemon Bliss Tea...103
Minty Ginger Green Tea..103
Chamomile Apple Zest Tea..104
Tropical Mango Bliss Smoothie...104
Berry Antioxidant Fusion...104
Green Goddess Smoothie...105
Classic Zesty Lemonade...105
Lavender Infused Lemonade..105
Sparkling Ginger Lemonade..106

Chapter 11: 4-Week Meal Plan 107

Tips for Success 108
Adjustments and Variations 108
Long-Term Tips and Strategies 109
1. Week 1: Getting Started 111
2. Week 2: Building Momentum 112
3. Week 3 & 4: Sustaining the DASH Lifestyle...113

Chapter 1: Understanding the DASH Diet

Welcome to a journey where your health takes center stage, but your busy schedule doesn't take a back seat. The DASH Diet, which stands for Dietary Approaches to Stop Hypertension, is not just a traditional diet—it's a lifelong approach to healthy eating designed to help control blood pressure without the rigidity that typically accompanies nutritional plans.

Picture this: you're navigating through the maze of modern food choices, where every shelf is laden with temptations that promise convenience at the cost of your wellbeing. It's here that DASH comes in as a beacon of hope, crafted based on years of research to combat high blood pressure, a silent adversary lurking in millions globally.

But, let's demystify something straightaway—the DASH Diet isn't merely about reducing the salt or avoiding specific food groups. Instead, it's a harmonious blending of nutrients that empowers your body to strengthen its defenses against hypertension and related issues. Think of it as recalibrating your eating habits to include more of what your body inherently craves for optimal health: fruits, vegetables, whole grains, and lean proteins, all playing vital roles in this dietary symphony.

What makes the DASH Diet particularly appealing, especially if you're juggling a hectic lifestyle, is its realistic, no-frills approach. It's flexible enough to adapt whether you're dining out, cooking a quick meal at home, or navigating a busy grocery store. This chapter will lay the groundwork, providing you with the essential knowledge to understand how and why the DASH Diet works. By integrating these principles, you're not just following a diet; you're embracing a healthier lifestyle choice that marries well with busy schedules and diverse family preferences.

So let's begin this journey with clarity and enthusiasm. You're not merely changing what's on your plate; you're embracing an approach that adjusts to your life's pace, understanding that each step forward is a step towards better health. Ready to take that first step? Let's delve deeper into understanding the DASH Diet and set the foundation for a nourishing path ahead.

1. WHAT IS THE DASH DIET?

Imagine a diet that not only promises to help manage your blood pressure but also transforms your overall eating habits into a healthful rhythm without feeling restrictive. That's the core of the DASH Diet, a plan initially sketched out by researchers who aimed to create a diet that would help lower blood pressure naturally, without the need for medication.

Origins and Benefits

The DASH Diet emerged from a series of studies in the early '90s. Funded by the National Institutes of Health, researchers sought to understand why certain populations had significantly lower incidence rates of hypertension compared to others. The common thread, they discovered, revolved around diet.

Unlike diets focusing solely on reducing salt intake, the DASH Diet emphasizes an increase in nutrients that help lower blood pressure, particularly potassium, calcium, and magnesium. By encouraging the consumption of fruits, vegetables, whole grains, and lean proteins, it aligns with a diet rich in these essential nutrients.

From a broader perspective, DASH isn't just about lowering blood pressure. It's also highly effective in reducing cholesterol levels, managing or preventing diabetes, and supporting heart health. This multifaceted approach makes it not only a medicinal strategy but also a preventive one, helping adherents maintain overall health and decrease the risk of many chronic diseases.

Scientific Evidence

Various studies have consistently supported the effectiveness of the DASH Diet. One pivotal study published in the New England Journal of Medicine demonstrated that participants who followed the DASH diet saw a significant drop in their systolic and diastolic blood pressure in just a few weeks. What sets these findings apart is that improvements were noted in various demographics, including different ages and health backgrounds, making DASH a universally applicable diet plan.

Further research has underscored its long-term benefits. For instance, following the DASH Diet has been linked to a reduced risk of developing heart disease by up to 20 percent and stroke by up to 29 percent. These statistics are compelling, especially in today's world where heart disease remains a leading cause of death globally.

How the DASH Diet Lowers Blood Pressure

The mechanics of how the DASH Diet lowers blood pressure is a fascinating synthesis of simple dietary adjustments that produce powerful results. At its heart, the reduction in blood pressure can be attributed to three major nutritional shifts:

1. **Increased Potassium Intake:** Potassium helps balance the amount of sodium in your cells, and not getting enough potassium can lead to high blood pressure. The DASH Diet promotes the intake of fruits and vegetables, which are natural sources of potassium, aiding in the excretion of sodium through urine and easing tension in the blood vessel walls.
2. **High Fiber Foods:** Fiber isn't just good for digestion—it's also associated with lower blood pressure. Foods rich in fiber, such as whole grains, help improve heart health by reducing blood cholesterol levels and providing a longer feeling of fullness, which can help with weight management.

3. **Limited Sodium and Saturated Fats:** By limiting the intake of sodium and foods high in saturated fats (like fatty meats and full-fat dairy products), the DASH Diet prevents the constriction of blood vessels while encouraging a heart-healthy profile.

Moreover, the emphasis on lean proteins and plant-based foods not only assists in controlling blood pressure but also supports a healthier metabolic state. This helps in mitigating other cardiovascular risk factors, creating a compound benefit.

In everyday terms, following the DASH Diet means you're equipping your body with what it needs to fight off high blood pressure naturally. Think of it as tuning an engine. Just as high-quality oil helps an engine run smoothly, a diet high in nutrients and low in unhealthy fats and sodium helps your cardiovascular system operate at its best.

In conclusion, the appeal of the DASH Diet lies in its simplicity and its direct approach to not just managing but also preventing high blood angle. It's a sustainable, evidence-based pathway to improved health that doesn't ask for drastic lifestyle changes, but rather, introduces wholesome, nutritious foods into your daily meals. Whether you're someone who is looking to lower your blood pressure, reduce cholesterol, or simply embrace a healthier lifestyle, the DASH Diet offers a feasible, scientifically backed blueprint that fits into any life story.

2. KEY PRINCIPLES OF THE DASH DIET

Embarking on the DASH Diet is like turning a new leaf in your book of dietary habits. Standing for Dietary Approaches to Stop Hypertension, this diet formulates a plan not just to combat high blood pressure but also to pave the way for a lifelong commitment to healthier eating. Understanding the key principles of this diet will help clarify why it has been so successful for so many and how its thoughtful approach can be seamlessly woven into daily life.

Recommended Food Groups

At the core of the DADSH Diet are the recommended food groups that provide the building blocks for its health benefits. This diet emphasizes a rich variety of nutrients sourced primarily from whole foods and minimally processed ingredients. Here are the cornerstone groups:

- **Fruits and Vegetables:** Laden with essential vitamins, minerals, and fibers, fruits and vegetables are the backbone of the DASH Diet. They not only help lower blood pressure but also contribute to overall health improvements, such as enhanced digestive health and better blood sugar control.
- **Whole Grains:** Moving away from refined grains to whole grains means benefiting from more fiber and nutrients. Whole grains help with digestion and maintain a steady blood sugar level, contributing to cardiovascular health.
- **Lean Proteins:** Including lean meats like poultry and fish, and extending to plant-based sources such as beans and legumes, lean proteins are critical. They provide essential amino acids without excessive saturated fat.
- **Low-fat Dairy:** By opting for low-fat or fat-free dairy products, adherence to the DASH Diet ensures intake of crucial calcium and vitamin D without the added risks of saturated fats, supporting bone and heart health.
- **Nuts, Seeds, and Healthy Fats:** Incorporating moderate amounts of unsalted nuts, seeds, and healthy fats like olive oil can enhance heart health by providing beneficial omega fatty acids and antioxidants.

Daily Nutrient Goals

Balancing nutrient intake is critical in the DASH Diet. Here's how the diet manages daily nutrition:

- **Sodium Reduction:** Given the direct link between sodium intake and blood pressure, reducing sodium is crucial. The DASH Diet typically recommends limiting sodium to about 2,300 milligrams per day, with an ideal limit of about 1,500 milligrams for most adults.
- **Potassium, Magnesium, and Calcium:** These three minerals aid in regulating blood pressure. The diet encourages foods high in these nutrients, aiming for a balanced intake that naturally counters the effects of sodium in the body.
- **Fiber:** High fiber intake is encouraged as it helps reduce blood cholesterol levels and fosters a feeling of fullness, assisting in weight management.
- **Lean Protein and Low Fat:** By emphasizing lean proteins and low-fat dairy, the diet restricts unhealthy fats, which contributes to the reduction of LDL (bad) cholesterol levels.

Portion Sizes and Serving Suggestions

Understanding portion sizes and proper serving suggestions is key to achieving success with the DASH Diet. Here's how you can manage your meal portions effectively:

- **Vegetables and Fruits:** Half of your plate should be vegetables and fruits at each meal. This not only ensures a lower calorie intake but also helps meet the daily fiber, vitamin, and mineral requirements.
- **Whole Grains:** About a quarter of your plate should consist of whole grains. This includes options like brown rice, whole wheat pasta, or quinoa.
- **Proteins:** The remaining quarter of your plate should be devoted to lean protein sources. This moderate portion helps manage calorie intake while providing essential nutrients.
- **Dairy:** Incorporate a serving or two of low-fat or fat-free dairy each day, which helps meet calcium and protein needs.
- **Nuts and Seeds:** A small handful of unsalted nuts or seeds can be an excellent daily addition, providing healthy fats and proteins.

The beauty of the DASH Diet is not in its rigidity but in its flexibility. It encourages a balanced approach to eating by focusing on nutrient-dense foods within appropriate portion sizes. This method helps create a sustainable dietary practice that can adjust to individual needs, preferences, and lifestyles.

Adopting the DASH Diet principles doesn't require a sweeping overhaul of your eating habits overnight. Rather, it's about making incremental changes that collectively contribute to significant health improvements. From choosing the right food groups to knowing how much and what to eat, the DASH Diet lays a firm foundation for those looking to manage their blood pressure and improve their overall health sustainably and effectively. Always remember, every meal is a step toward a healthier you. By understanding and integrating these principles, you are not just following a diet; you are embracing a healthier lifestyle that supports long-term well-being.

3. GETTING STARTED

Embarking on the DASH Diet journey may feel like sailing into uncharted waters especially if your current dietary habits are a far cry from what DASH proposes. Fear not—starting is about taking those initial, perhaps tentative, steps towards embracing a healthier lifestyle that aims not just at lowering your blood pressure but also enhancing your overall health. Let's explore how to set the course right from assessing your present eating habits to overcoming the inevitable early challenges.

Assessing Your Current Diet

Before we can map out where we're going, we need to understand where we stand. This involves taking a deep and honest look at your existing diet. Start by keeping a food diary for a week. Write down everything you eat and drink, noting the approximate quantities and the time of day. This isn't about judging yourself but about establishing a baseline from which you can grow.

Observe patterns: Are you skipping meals? Do you lean heavily on snacks or fast food? How often do you eat fruits and vegetables? Often, just the act of writing things down can illuminate habits you might not have been aware of, such as a tendency to eat out of boredom or stress rather than hunger.

Setting Realistic Goals

With a clear view of your current eating habits, the next step would be setting achievable, realistic goals. This is crucial. Overambitious goals can lead to frustration and setbacks. Here, the DASH Diet shines as it accommodates flexibility. Initially, you might focus on achievable objectives like incorporating a serving of vegetables in each meal or reducing your intake of processed foods and sweets gradually.

Setting short-term goals can be as simple as deciding, for a week, to replace dessert with a fruit or choosing water over soda. Celebrate these small victories—they build confidence and momentum. As you grow comfortable, these shorter-term goals can evolve into long-term commitments, such as achieving and maintaining the dietary sodium intake recommendations of the DASH Diet.

Overcoming Initial Challenges

Change isn't easy, and dietary changes are no exception. One of the first hurdles might be a craving for salt if you're used to high-sodium foods. Overcoming this can be as simple as discovering the natural flavors in fresh produce or using herbs and spices instead of salt for seasoning. Remember, taste is adaptable; your palate can learn to enjoy less salt over time.

Another common challenge is time. Integrating a diet full of fruits, vegetables, and whole grains might seem time-consuming—especially if you're used to quicker, more convenient meals. Here, planning is your ally. Setting aside time each week to plan meals, prepare ingredients, or even batch-cook dishes can turn what seems like a daunting task into a manageable part of your routine.

You might also face resistance from family members, particularly if dietary habits are deeply ingrained or if there are picky eaters in the household. Including them in the process can be beneficial. Let them choose some of the new vegetables to try or involve them in the meal preparation. Make it an adventure rather than a mandate, focusing on the variety and flavors they enjoy.

As you tackle these challenges, keep your eyes on the prize: improved health. Each small dietary adjustment is a step towards reducing your blood pressure and enhancing your overall wellbeing. The journey will require adjustments and patience, but with each step, you will be reinforcing a healthier lifestyle that not only aligns with the DASH Diet but also sits well with your personal life and preferences.

Starting the DASH Diet doesn't have to feel like an insurmountable challenge. By assessing your current eating habits, setting realistic goals, and gradually overcoming the initial obstacles, you prepare yourself for a successful journey towards better health. As with any voyage, there might be obstacles, but the destination—a healthier, more vibrant you—is well worth the journey.

CHAPTER 2: ESSENTIAL ALIMENTARY TIPS

Embarking on the DASH diet journey, you've acquainted yourself with its fundamental aspects—what it is and why it's beneficial. Now, let's navigate through the next crucial step: mastering your alimentary choices. In this chapter, we'll explore essential tips that make adopting this wholesome diet an easy integration into your lifestyle, regardless of your bustling schedule.

Picture your weekly grocery run: the aisles brimming with products, some beaming health claims that seem too good to be true. Here, the skill of smart shopping becomes your best ally. I'll guide you on how to pick the freshest produce, the leanest meats, and the most beneficial grains, all while avoiding the common traps that can set back your health goals. Our objective? To fill your cart with choices that are as nutritious as they are delicious.

Meal prep might conjure images of your kitchen strewn with various pots and pans, a time-consuming Sunday ritual. Let's dismantle that notion. Visualize instead the serene simplicity of having your weekly meals planned and prepped within a couple of hours—a practical approach to cooking that respects your time constraints and energy levels.

The tale doesn't end at making smart choices and meal prepping. Decoding food labels is akin to understanding a new language, one that, once learned, can empower you significantly. Have you ever turned a package around and wondered what all those percentages and terms mean? We'll demystify this together, turning confusion into clarity. From spotting hidden sugars to understanding what 'low-fat' really implies, your newfound knowledge will turn you into a savvy shopper in no time.

These alimentary tips are not just strategies; they are transformative practices that enhance your relationship with food. They ensure that your journey on the DASH diet is not just about adhering to dietary guidelines but truly enjoying and savoring the art of eating well. Let's embark on this path not just with the goal of longevity but for a vibrant life filled with flavorful, heart-healthy meals.

1. Smart Shopping for the DASH Diet

Imagine strolling through the grocery store with a new sense of purpose and expertise. You're not just shopping; you're strategically selecting foods that enhance your health, fit your busy lifestyle, and align perfectly with the Directions Approach to Stop Hypertension (DASH) diet. This isn't about restricting your culinary pleasures but about making smarter choices that are both satisfying and beneficial.

Creating a DASH-Friendly Grocery List

The foundation of smart shopping on the DASH diet begins long before you enter the store—it starts at home with a well-thought-out grocery list. This list isn't just a reminder of what to buy; it serves as a blueprint for your nutritional goals. Focus on including a variety of foods that are rich in potassium, calcium, fiber, and protein, while low in sodium and saturated fat. This means your list will prominently feature fruits, vegetables, whole grains, lean proteins, and low-fat dairy products.

Start by writing down staples that fit into the DASH diet, such as oats, brown rice, and whole wheat pasta for your carbohydrate sources. Then, add various fruits like berries, apples, and bananas which are not only heart-healthy but also keep you fuller for longer. Vegetables should make up a large portion of your list—think leafy greens, bell peppers, and sweet potatoes, all vibrant in color and packed with essential nutrients.

Proteins should be lean. Consider white meats like turkey and chicken, fish rich in omega-3 fatty acids like salmon, and plant-based sources such as beans and lentils. Don't forget about seeds and nuts, which make excellent snacks and can add crunch and nutrition to your meals.

Lastly, dairy or its alternatives should be low-fat or fat-free. Options like Greek yogurt, skim milk, or almond milk offer excellent sources of calcium without the added saturated fat.

Shopping on a Budget

Adhering to the DASH diet doesn't mean you have to increase your grocery bill. There are plenty of ways to stick to your budget while making health-conscious choices. One of the most effective strategies is to prioritize buying generic or store brands for staples like rice, pasta, and canned vegetables. These products are often identical in quality to their branded counterparts but at a fraction of the cost.

Bulk buying is another way to save money. Items such as dried beans, rice, and certain spices are usually available in bulk and can be much cheaper than pre-packaged versions. However, be mindful of the shelf life and storage options to avoid wastage.

Seasonal shopping is a budget-friendly tip that aligns well with buying the freshest produce. Fruits and vegetables are generally less expensive when they are in season and are at their nutritional peak. Plus, they taste better too, making them more enjoyable to eat.

Another tip is to scan flyers and apps for sales and coupons. Planning your meals around what is on sale that week can help lower costs significantly. Moreover, embracing a flexible approach to your grocery list allows you to make adjustments based on what items are discounted without compromising the quality of your diet.

Choosing the Best Produce

Selecting the best produce means looking for freshness and ripeness, which directly impact both the taste and the nutritional value of your meals. When choosing fruits, look for pieces that are firm, have a vibrant color, and are free from bruises or blemishes. Smell can also be a strong indicator of ripeness—fragrant fruits are often ready to eat.

For vegetables, the rules are similar. Fresh vegetables generally have a crisp texture, rich color, and are free from soft spots or wilting. Green leafy vegetables should look vibrant and perky, not limp or browned.

Understanding the labels on produce can also enhance your shopping experience. Terms like "organic" refer to how the fruits and vegetables were grown, without synthetic pesticides or genetic modifications. While organic produce is a great option, it can be more expensive. Weigh the benefits against your budget, and remember that the main goal is to increase your intake of fruits and vegetables, regardless of their organic status.

In some cases, frozen or canned fruits and vegetables can be just as nutritious as fresh varieties, especially if they are processed at their peak ripeness. These options can be more affordable and provide off-season varieties all year round. For canned goods, look for products with no added salt or sugars to keep in line with DASH diet recommendations.

By integrating these strategies—crafting a smart, DASH-friendly grocery list, shopping wisely to adhere to your budget, and selecting the best produce—you transform your shopping routine into a health-forward, cost-effective practice. This approach not only aligns with the DASH diet principles but also supports a sustainable lifestyle change, making healthy eating both achievable and enjoyable, no matter your schedule.

2. Meal Prep Made Easy

Meal prepping is the secret sauce to maintaining a heart-healthy DASH diet amidst your bustling lifestyle. It's about more than just chopping vegetables and packaging meals; it's a thoughtful routine that ensures you consistently feed your body the nourishing foods it craves without demanding significant daily time investments. Let's walk through how to turn your kitchen efforts into a smooth, efficient, and enjoyable process.

Efficient Meal Prep Strategies

Goal-setting is paramount. Start each week by mapping out what you'd like to eat. This doesn't need to be a rigid menu but a flexible guideline that allows you to accommodate unexpected changes in your week. Ask yourself: What meals do I enjoy that align with the DASH diet? How varied is my diet? Am I getting enough of each macronutrient? Planning with these questions in mind ensures you maintain dietary balance and eliminate the daily "what's for dinner?" dilemma, reducing stress and poor food choices.

Once your weekly meals are outlined, consolidate your cooking processes. Think about how you can cook a base that's versatile. For example, preparing a large batch of quinoa can serve as a foundation for a stir-fry dish one night, a hearty salad the next day, and perhaps a savory breakfast porridge. This method reduces time and keeps your meals interesting.

Incorporate overlapping ingredients across different meals. If multiple meals call for diced carrots, chop them all at once to save time later. This approach minimizes waste and streamlines your cooking process, keeping you efficient and focused.

Ensure your meal prep day is marked on your calendar as a recurring event. Treat this time as a priority—equivalent to a meeting or appointment. This habit not only cements the routine but also mentally prepares you to invest in your health regularly.

Essential Kitchen Tools

The right tools can transform meal preparation from a chore into a pleasure. A high-quality chef's knife and a sturdy cutting board will make chopping and dicing more efficient and safer. Invest in a set of glass storage containers; not only do they allow you to see your beautifully prepared meals at a glance, but they are also better for reheating food than plastic alternatives.

A slow cooker or a pressure cooker is invaluable for preparing bulk meals with minimal effort. These appliances work wonders for cooking legumes, stews, and lean meats, infusing flavors deeply and tenderly. Additionally, a good blender makes smoothies and soups a breeze, offering a quick meal solution that does not compromise on nutrition.

Don't overlook the convenience of silicone baking sheets and muffin pans, essential for making meal components like breakfast cups or portion-controlled snacks. These tools are naturally nonstick, reducing the need for added oils and making cleanup effortless.

Batch Cooking Tips

Batch cooking is an effective tactic to ensure you have nutritious meals on hand throughout the week. When preparing meals in large quantities, consider how each component will reheat. Some ingredients, like certain fish or delicate vegetables, are best cooked fresh or added last during the reheating process to maintain texture and flavor.

When portioning meals, think about your weekly schedule. On busier days, you might benefit from more grab-and-go options like pre-made salads or wraps, while evenings at home might allow for quick heat-and-eat meals like soups or stews.

Cool foods properly before storage to maintain safety and quality. Spread out hot foods on large, shallow pans to allow them to cool quickly and evenly before transferring them to your fridge or freezer. This process helps preserve the freshness and prevents the growth of bacteria.

Label your containers with the date of preparation. This practice not only helps with rotating your stock but also ensures that you consume your meals while they are at their peak freshness and flavor.

Finally, embrace flexibility. While consistency is key, life's unpredictable nature means adjustments will be necessary. Sometimes you might swap meals between days, or opt for a quick, healthy alternative if time constraints demand it. What matters most is that you are creating a sustainable habit of eating well, aligned with the DASH diet principles.

By equipping yourself with a solid plan, the right tools, and practical batch cooking techniques, meal prepping becomes less of a daily hurdle and more of a weekly triumph over your time and health. This approach not only supports your DASH diet adherence but also buffers you against the stress of unprepared meal times, making your health goals an achievable part of your everyday routine.

3. READING FOOD LABELS

Navigating the maze of food labels can often feel like deciphering a complex code. However, understanding these labels is key to making informed, health-conscious choices that align with the DASH diet. Whether you are managing hypertension or simply aiming for a healthier lifestyle, grasping the nuances of nutritional information can empower you and transform your approach to grocery shopping.

Understanding Nutritional Information

Every packaged food comes with a label that provides valuable insights into its nutritional content. Learning to read and understand this information ensures that you can choose foods that contribute positively to your heart health and overall well-being.

Start with the serving size, which sets the stage for interpreting everything else on the label. All the nutritional values that follow are based on this amount, so if you consume less or more, you'll need to adjust these figures accordingly. Remember, what might seem like a small package could contain multiple servings, which can be misleading if you're not mindful.

Next, pay attention to the calories per serving. Calories are a measure of how much energy you get from a serving of the food. Balancing the calories you consume from foods and beverages with the calories you expend through physical activity is fundamental to maintaining a healthy weight.

The nutrients listed next are what you should limit: sodium, saturated fat, trans fat, and cholesterol. High intake of these can lead to an increased risk of chronic conditions like heart disease and high blood pressure. The DASH diet particularly emphasizes reducing sodium intake, so this should be a number you look at closely.

Fiber, vitamins, and minerals usually follow on the label. These are the nutrients you want to consume in greater amounts. Dietary fiber, for instance, not only aids digestion but also helps to regulate blood sugar and cholesterol levels—key components in managing blood pressure.

Identifying Hidden Sodium and Sugars

Sodium is often sneakily high in seemingly healthy foods like canned vegetables, bread, and soups. When shopping, aim for items labeled "low sodium" or "no salt added." This signifies that the food contains far less sodium than its regular counterpart. However, be vigilant and read the actual sodium content on the nutrition label, as definitions of "low" can vary.

Sugars also lurk under various aliases—fructose, lactose, sucrose, maltose, glucose, and high-fructose corn syrup, to name a few. Watch out for these, especially in foods where you might not expect to find sugar, like salad dressings and sauces. The DASH diet encourages minimizing your intake of added sugars, which can contribute to weight gain and hinder your heart health.

In addition to sugars, additives and preservatives are other components to be aware of. While not all are harmful, some, like MSG (monosodium glutamate), can subtly increase sodium levels in the body.

Making Healthier Choices

Empowered with the knowledge of how to read food labels, you can make choices that are better aligned with your health goals. Here are some practical tips to incorporate into your shopping routine:

- **Choose more whole foods**: Fruits, vegetables, and grains in their natural or whole form generally contain no hidden salts, sugars, or unhealthy fats. They are also rich in dietary fiber and essential nutrients that processed foods often lack.
- **Opt for balance and variety**: Focus on buying a range of foods to ensure a balanced diet. This helps in covering all nutritional bases and keeps your meals interesting.
- **Be cautious with 'diet' foods**: Just because a product is marketed as being good for weight loss doesn't necessarily mean it's healthier. Sometimes, to compensate for reduced fat or calories, the sugar or sodium content might be higher.
- **Prepare for your shopping trips**: Having a list reduces the risk of impulse buys, which are often less healthy options. Spend more time in the perimeter of the store where fresh foods like fruits, vegetables, and lean proteins are typically located.

By understanding food labels and making mindful food selections, you turn every trip to the grocery store into a mission for better health. This knowledge acts as your shield, protecting you from the pitfalls of hidden sodium, sugars, and unhealthy fats. With each mindful choice, you're steps closer to maintaining a balanced, heart-healthy diet that resonates with the core principles of the DASH diet, ensuring that you not only follow a diet but embrace a lifestyle that sustains your health and vitality.

CHAPTER 3: MANAGING SODIUM INTAKE

Navigating the supermarket aisles, reading labels, and making sense of what's high in sodium and what's not can feel like deciphering an ancient code. But why this fuss about sodium? Sodium definitely has a role to play in our body, helping to control blood pressure and fluid balance. However, the pinch of salt that turns into multiple pinches over the day can lead the scale to tip disturbingly towards high blood pressure, a silent partner in crime to heart diseases.

Managing your sodium intake isn't about bland food or drastic measures. It's about striking a balance. Picture this: you are at your favorite restaurant staring down a menu that's mouth-watering but potentially a sodium minefield. Or in the kitchen, ready to whip up a quick dinner. The reality is, you can handle these situations with ease and confidence once you know the secrets behind sodium management.

Think about the pleasure of savoring a freshly prepared meal that you know is good for you and your family's health. In this chapter, we explore the realms where sodium lurks and master the art of manipulating it to our benefit—turning every meal into a heart-healthy feast. We'll start by understanding why minding sodium matters. Ever wondered how to cook low-sodium meals that still explode with flavors or how to make smart choices when dining out? You're not alone!

With a few tweaks to your cooking techniques, a dash of creativity in flavoring, and smart choices, you can significantly reduce your sodium intake without sacrificing taste. We'll embark on this journey together, from the grocery store to the dinner table, to confidently create meals that delight both the palate and the heart. This chapter will be your guide to a salter strategy for a healthier life. So, let's turn the page on high sodium habits and start a fresh chapter on managing your intake with savvy and style, proving that a lower-sodium life can indeed be delicious and effortless.

1. Why Sodium Matters

Understanding the role of sodium in your diet is like unraveling a crucial thread in the fabric of your overall health, particularly when it revolves around blood pressure management. For many, sodium is just another element on the periodic table or simply a component of table salt; but when you delve deeper, you begin to see its significant impact on bodily functions and overall well-being.

The Impact of Sodium on Blood Appeal

Sodium chloride, which you know as salt, plays pivotal roles in our body. It helps maintain cellular function, fluid balance, and is crucial in nerve transmission and muscle contraction. However, the story takes a twist when excess sodium starts accumulating. This surplus doesn't just sit idle; it pulls water into your bloodstream, increasing the total volume of blood inside your veins. Like a garden hose that swells under high water pressure, your blood vessels bear the brunt of this extra volume, subsequently raising your blood pressure.

Elevated blood pressure isn't a trivial issue. It forces your heart to work harder to pump blood through your vessels, contributing to hardening and narrowing of arteries, and eventually leading to heart diseases, strokes, and kidney problems. It's a silent threat, often presenting no clear symptoms but steadily chipping away at your health, making the control of sodium intake not just beneficial, but essential for long-term health and quality of life.

Recommended Sodium Limits

Guidelines from leading health authorities like the American Heart Association suggest that adults should aim for no more than 2,300 milligrams of sodium per day. That's about one teaspoon of table salt. Yet, ideal limits are set even lower at 1,500 milligrams for those who are more susceptible to the effects of sodium—like those with hypertension, individuals over age 50, or those of African descent. Despite these recommendations, the average American consumes about 3,400 milligrams daily, substantially higher than recommended levels.

Understanding these numbers exposes a gap between our current dietary habits and what is considered healthy. Closing this gap doesn't require monumental changes but a series of informed, manageable choices. Reducing sodium intake to recommended levels can significantly lower blood pressure, which decreases the risk of developing heart complications.

Common High-Sodium Foods to Avoid

You might think that most of your sodium intake comes from the salt shaker. However, up to 75% of the sodium we consume is hidden in processed foods and restaurant meals—far away from the realms of our salt shakers. Recognizing and reducing these hidden sources is a key step in managing sodium intake.

1. **Processed and Prepackaged Foods**: These are notorious for their high sodium content. Canned soups, frozen dinners, and cured meats like bacon and deli meats are laden with sodium, used in these products not only to enhance flavor but also to preserve them. The convenience they offer on a busy night or during a rushed morning is undeniable, but the sodium cost is high.
2. **Snacks**: Chips, pretzels, popcorn, and other savory snacks are moreish but often come with a generous sodium topping. It's easy to nibble through a whole bag unconsciously, and by doing so, deeply dent your sodium quota for the day.
3. **Condiments and Sauces**: It's not just about what you cook, but also about how you flavor it. Soy sauce, ketchup, mayonnaise, and salad dressings can stealthily introduce high levels of sodium to seemingly healthy meals. Opting for low-sodium versions or using herbs and spices for flavoring can dramatically cut your sodium intake.

4. **Breads and Rolls**: Though they don't taste salty, bread, and rolls consistently rank as high contributors to sodium intake. This is due to both their sodium content and their prevalence in our diets. Checking labels and choosing lower-sodium options can help mitigate this exposure.
5. **Restaurant Food**: Dining out can be a hidden source of excessive sodium. Restaurant dishes are often high in sodium to enhance flavor and appeal broadly. You can harness control by requesting dishes to be made with less salt, or better opt for items that are steamed, grilled, or baked using natural herbs and spices.

Managing sodium involves being aware of its impacts, understanding the daily limits, and identifying high-sodium foods to avoid or limit. Tackling this doesn't mean you're destined for dull and tasteless meals. Instead, with awareness and a few smart choices, you'll find that reducing sodium intake can align well with a flavorful and satisfying eating pattern. With this knowledge, you can take proactive steps to ensure that your diet supports a heart-healthy lifestyle, leading to a more energetic, healthier you without the weight of excess sodium.

2. Low-Sodium Cooking Techniques

Embracing a low-sodium lifestyle does not invariably equate to compromising on flavor. The artistry of cooking is vibrantly omnipresent—particularly when creativity is summoned to offset the reduced use of salt. Revolutionizing your kitchen practices to favor low-sodium cooking techniques is less about stripping away flavors and more about enhancing the natural savoriness of ingredients, allowing them to shine through innovative uses of herbs, spices, and other flavor-packed, healthier alternatives.

Flavoring Foods Without Salt

The culinary challenge of reducing salt can be mastered by exploiting the intrinsic flavors of food through cooking methods that amplify their natural essence without the need for excessive seasoning. Techniques such as grilling, roasting, and slow cooking caramelize the natural sugars in foods, deepening flavors naturally. For instance, grilling vegetables or roasting a chicken are simple processes, but they focus the natural flavors, creating complex, rich profiles that salt is often mistakenly believed to be necessary to achieve.

Engaging in the practice of using acidic ingredients like lemon juice, lime, or vinegar can also elevate a dish's taste profile. These elements add a clean, sharp brightness that can mimic the flavor-enhancing property of salt. A dash of vinegar or a squeeze of fresh lemon juice just before serving can transform a seemingly flat dish into a vibrant culinary experience.

Using Herbs and Spices

The strategic use of herbs and spices stands as one of the pillars of low-sodium cooking. Each herb and spice holds unique potential to bring a dish to life. Consider creating various blends that can be used across multiple dishes: - For a touch of warmth and sweetness, cinnamon, nutmeg, and clove offer deep, aromatic accents. - For brightness and lightness, consider the zesty punch of basil, cilantro, or parsley. - Smoked paprika, cumin, and black pepper bring robustness and depth, easily stepping in to fill the gap left by reduced salt.

Crafting your own herb and spice blends not only personalizes your cooking but also sidesteps the hidden sodium often found in prepackaged seasoning mixes. Refreshing a culinary arsenal with a variety of spices can unleash a new level of creativity in your cooking routine.

Low-Sodium Alternatives and Substitutes

Replacing certain ingredient with low-sodium alternatives is another strategic approach. Instead of standard table salt, consider utilizing salt substitutes or reduced-sodium salts which contain potassium chloride — though this should be used cautiously, especially for those with kidney issues or those who require restricted potassium diets.

Beyond salt substitutes, consider these modifications: - Opt for unsalted or low-sodium versions of broths and stocks or make your own to control the sodium content. - Replace regular cheeses with lower-sodium varieties, or use stronger-flavored cheeses like Parmesan or feta sparingly for a salty effect. - In recipes calling for creamy textures, use alternatives like Greek yogurt in place of sour cream or mayonnaise to cut down on sodium.

The use of rubs and marinades can tenderize and enrich meats without heavy salt content. By allowing meat to marinate for several hours or even overnight in a blend of spices, herbs, and acidic components, you not only infuse the meat with intense flavor but also improve its texture and moisture content, reducing the need for salt.

Practical Tips to Implement Low-Sodium Cooking Techniques Everyday

Implementing a low-sodium diet is about making small, manageable changes rather than drastic overhauls. Begin by: - Gradually reducing the salt used in recipes to allow your taste buds to adjust. - Increasing the ratio of herbs and spices to replace the flavor spectrum that salt would normally provide. - Using natural extracts and zests, like vanilla or citrus zest, to enhance sweetness and flavor without added sugars or salt. - Exploring international cuisines known for their adept use of spices, such as Mediterranean or Indian, which are often flavorful without relying heavily on salt.

With these strategies, your journey to a low-sodium lifestyle can become not only a healthy choice but a delightful culinary adventure. Embracing the array of flavors that nature offers, you can enjoy rich, robust meals that support your health, tease your palate, and satisfy your dietary needs without an over-reliance on salt. This thoughtful approach to cooking promises a diet that is as nourishing as it is delicious, proving that less sodium in your diet can bring more enjoyment to your table.

3. DINING OUT ON THE DASH DIET

Strolling into a restaurant, the aromas, ambiance, and the promise of a meal crafted by someone else can feel like a true delight—an indulgence in the daily routine of life. Yet for those committed to a DASH lifestyle, the question looms: How can you indulge without straying from your low-sodium intentions? The good news is that dining out can still be a joyous, delicious, and heart-healthy experience with the right know-how and a bit of proactive planning.

Tips for Eating Out Healthily

The key to successfully managing your sodium intake while enjoying a meal out is preparation. Before even stepping into a restaurant, research is crucial. Most establishments have menus available online, complete with nutritional information that allows the savvy diner to scout out safe options in advance. Websites and mobile apps dedicated to nutrition can help decipher which dishes are loaded with sodium and which are more in line with the DASH diet.

Once you arrive at the restaurant, don't hesitate to engage the server in a conversation about the menu. Inquire about the preparation methods of dishes that interest you, request modifications where necessary, and ask for sauces or dressings to be served on the side so you can control the amount you consume.

Making Smart Menu Choices

Navigating the menu thoughtfully is another vital skill. Look for keywords that suggest less processed food such as "steamed," "grilled," "baked" or "roasted." These cooking methods typically use less oil and salt. On the other hand, terms like "pickled," "brined," "cured," and "smoked" are indicators of high sodium content.

Opting for dishes dominated by fresh vegetables, lean proteins, and whole grains is always a smart choice. These ingredients are naturally lower in sodium and align well with the DASH diet principles. If ordering a salad, ask for leafy greens and a variety of vegetables, topped with grilled chicken, fish, or legumes, all dressed with a splash of olive oil and vinegar or lemon juice instead of pre-made dressings.

Handling Social Situations

Social dining is all about enjoyment, which includes both the food and the company. Balance is key—not just in what you eat, but also in how you manage social expectations and pressures. When dining with others, focus on the joy of their company rather than the limitations of your diet. You can participate fully without drawing unnecessary attention to your dietary restrictions.

If you're choosing a restaurant with a group, suggest a place that you know has a variety of healthy options. When ordering, you can make it a seamless part of the conversation. Simply state what modifications you'd like clearly and politely to the server. Often, friends and family are curious or even inspired by your dedication to health, turning what could be a challenge into an opportunity to share your journey and maybe encourage others to think about their own dietary choices.

Handling the inevitable temptations requires a blend of firmness and flexibility. Decide in advance how strictly you need to adhere to your low-sodium goals. If it's a special occasion, you might choose to allow yourself a slight deviation from your diet, but be strategic about it—perhaps by compensating with a particularly healthy meal earlier in the day.

Additional Strategies for Success

To further ensure you stay on track, here are a few more strategies: - Start your meal with a glass of water or a salad (with dressing on the side) to temper your appetite. - Share a dish with someone if portion sizes are large, or ask the server to box up half the meal before it even reaches the table. - Choose fruit for dessert or a dairy-based dessert like a plain sorbet, which are typically lower in sodium than other dessert options.

These strategies empower you to maintain control over your sodium intake while enjoying the social and culinary pleasures of dining out. Restaurants can accommodate dietary preferences more than ever before, and by employing foresight and clear communication, you can protect your heart health without sacrificing your social life. This balanced approach allows you to cherish both your health goals and your valued relationships, making each dining experience a fulfilling part of your journey on the DASH diet.

CHAPTER 4: BALANCING MACRONUTRIENTS

Welcome to a fascinating journey through the world of macronutrients: those vital nutrients that fuel our daily lives, shaping our health and wellness. Think of balancing macronutrients as tuning a magnificent, complex instrument—your body, to play the sweetest melodies of health and vitality.

Imagine your daily diet as a canvas, macronutrients are the colors you'll use to paint your masterpiece. You've likely heard about proteins, fats, and carbohydrates, but understanding how to harmoniously balance these in your meals can transform your approach to eating, especially within the guidelines of the DASH diet.

Protein, the building block of life, lends strength to your muscles and bones. It's like the sturdy frame that supports the structure of your diet. Carbohydrates, often misunderstood, are the primary source of energy for the body, fueling everything from brain function to physical activity—think of them as the vibrant splashes of color that bring energy to your painting. And fats, far from being foes, act as a rich gloss, giving depth and sustainability to your energy, aiding absorption of vital vitamins, and enhancing food flavors.

Now, you might wonder how you can manage these macronutrients effectively in your daily meals. It's simpler than you might think! The key is not just in choosing the right kinds of each macronutrient—whole grains for carbohydrates, lean proteins, and healthy fats like avocados and nuts—but in understanding their proportions and how they can complement each other.

For instance, blending a balance of macronutrients at dinner might look like a grilled salmon fillet (rich in protein and healthy fats), a side of quinoa (a wonderful source of proteins and carbohydrates), and a vibrant salad dressed with olive oil (hello, healthy fats!). Such a meal doesn't just satiate your taste buds but also aligns beautifully with your body's health requirements.

As we delve deeper into this chapter, keep in mind that mastering macronutrients on the DASH diet is not just about meticulous counting or strict limitations. It's about creating a flexible, enjoyable, and sustainable way to nourish your body, ensuring you relish your meals while keeping your heart healthy and your energy levels buoyant. Let's explore how you can craft delicious, balanced dishes that make every meal an opportunity for wellness and satisfaction.

1. Understanding Macronutrients

Every bite you take is more than just food; it's a complex interplay of fuels and nutrients that power your body's many functions. Understanding macronutrients—carbohydrates, proteins, and fats—lays the groundwork for building a nourishing, heart-healthy diet that aligns with the DASH lifestyle. Let's unwrap these critical components, how they function in the body, and how balancing them can elevate your overall health.

The Role of Carbohydrates, Proteins, and Fats

Carbohydrates often get a bad rap, but they are the primary energy source for the brain and body. Reflect on a time when you felt sluggish until you had a bite to eat; chances are, carbs played a hero role in revitalizing you. They come in various forms, from the sugars in your morning orange juice to the starches in potatoes and grainy goodness of whole bread. Complex carbohydrates, such as those found in whole grains, fruits, and vegetables, are studded with fiber, helping slow digestion and giving you a more stable energy release. This fiber also aids in digestion and supports heart health by helping to manage cholesterol levels.

Protein, on the other hand, functions as the building block for your muscles, skin, enzymes, and hormones. It maintains the body's growth, repairs tissues, and supports immune function. Think of a time when you recovered from a cut or bruise; protein played a pivotal role in healing that wound. Animal products like fish, poultry, and beef are rich in this macronutrient, but plant-based sources such as beans, quinoa, and nuts are equally important contributors, especially beneficial in a DASH diet.

Fats have traditionally been viewed through a lens of caution, but understanding the diversity among types of fats can change this perception. While you should minimize saturated and trans fats, monounsaturated and polyunsaturated fats — found in olive oil, avocados, and fish — boost heart health by lowering bad cholesterol levels and raising good cholesterol. Additionally, these healthy fats are necessary for absorbing fat-soluble vitamins A, D, E, and K, which keep your eyes, skin, lungs, gastrointestinal tract, and nervous system in check.

Balanced Meals for Optimal Health

Visualize your plate as a palette of colors, each representing different macronutrients, contributing unique and vital nutrients. For optimum health, each meal should contain a balance of carbohydrates, proteins, and fats. This not only supports varied bodily functions but also aids in sustaining fullness and satisfaction after meals, which is crucial for managing weight and preventing hypertension.

Consider a typical dinner plate filled half with vegetables (rich in fibrous carbohydrates), one-quarter with lean protein (like grilled chicken or tofu), and another quarter with a whole grain (like brown rice or quinoa), topped with a drizzle of olive oil (a healthy fat). This balance helps stabilize blood sugar levels, keeps you fuller longer, and provides a steady energy release, all of which are core advantages in managing blood pressure and supporting heart health.

Adjusting Macronutrient Ratios

The beautiful thing about the human body is its uniqueness from one individual to another, which means macronutrient needs can vary based on total energy expenditure, metabolic health, physical activity, and even personal goals like weight loss or muscle gain. Initially, the DASH diet emphasizes proportions similar to what was described: about half your calories from carbohydrates, one quarter from protein, and another quarter from fats, with a focus on the healthy varieties of each.

However, some might find they thrive on a slightly higher protein intake, especially if they're older or more active, as protein can help preserve muscle mass and strength. Others might need more healthy fats for specific health reasons, or less total carbohydrate intake if managing blood sugar is a priority.

Experimenting under the guidance of healthcare providers like dietitians can help fine-tune these ratios, creating a tailored approach that fits seamlessly into your life and meets your specific health needs. Remember, the goal of the DASH diet isn't to restrict joyously eating but to find a way of eating that feels good, supports bodily health, and is sustainable long-term.

Understanding and integrating the knowledge of macronutrients in your daily diet empowers you with the tool to not only achieve optimal health but also enjoy food's pleasure. As you continue through this book, let this foundational knowledge inspire your meal planning and preparation, helping you craft not just meals but a vibrant, flavor-filled lifestyle that keeps your heart beating at its happiest.

2. HEALTHY CARBOHYDRATES

In our quest for a heart-healthy life, understanding carbohydrates—their forms and functions—is pivotal, especially when following the philosophy of the DASH diet. Carbohydrates are often painted as dietary villains, but the truth is, they're essential to our health, providing the primary source of energy our bodies need to function at their best. Let's embark on a journey to explore 'healthy carbohydrates', focusing on whole grains and fiber, the bountiful benefits of fruits and vegetables, and strategies for reducing refined sugars in our diet.

Whole Grains and Fiber

Think of whole grains as the unsung heroes of the carbohydrate family. Unlike their refined counterparts, whole grains are packed with nutrients because they contain all parts of the grain kernel—the bran, germ, and endosperm. This means they provide more fiber, protein, and a host of vitamins and minerals that are often lost during the refining process.

Fiber, a critical component of whole grains, offers a cascade of health benefits. It helps to slow the absorption of sugar, aiding in blood sugar control, and it increases satiety, which can prevent overeating. High fiber intake is also linked to a lower risk of heart disease, mainly because it helps to reduce cholesterol levels and promotes a healthy digestive system.

Including whole grains in your diet doesn't have to be a chore. Foods like oats, brown rice, barley, and whole-wheat bread are not only nutritious but incredibly versatile. From morning oatmeal loaded with fresh berries to a hearty barley soup, whole grains can be delicious staples in your DASH diet-friendly kitchen.

Benefits of Fruits and Vegetables

Moving along in our journey of carbohydrates, let's talk about fruits and vegetables—nature's own medicine filled with vitamins, minerals, fiber, and antioxidants. These components are vital in combatting inflammation, which is linked to a myriad of chronic diseases including hypertension and heart conditions.

Consuming a diverse range of fruits and vegetables ensures a variety of nutrients that support different body functions. For example, the potassium found abundantly in bananas and potatoes can help manage blood pressure levels, while the antioxidants in berries and leafy greens may protect your heart and boost brain health. Integrating more fruits and vegetables into your diet can be both enjoyable and creative. Whether it's adding spinach to your morning smoothie, snacking on carrot sticks and hummus, or tossing a colorful salad with dinner, these foods can easily become a regular part of your eating plan. Remember, the more color on your plate, the broader the spectrum of nutrients you're feeding your body.

Reducing Refined Sugars

As we embrace whole grains and bountiful fruits and vegetables, another topic needs our attention: refined sugars. These sugars are stripped of nutritional value during processing and can rapidly spike blood glucose levels, leading to energy crashes and various health issues over time. Reducing refined sugars is crucial for maintaining a balanced diet and protecting your heart health.

Cutting back on refined sugars involves making mindful choices about what you eat. Start by reading food labels carefully—sugars hide under many names like sucrose, high-fructose corn syrup, and dextrose. Also, consider reducing your consumption of sweets, sodas, and even fruit juices, which can contain concentrated sugar.

Instead of these sugary options, try satisfying your sweet tooth with whole fruits, which provide natural sugars along with fiber and essential nutrients. Experimenting with spices like cinnamon and nutmeg, as well as flavors like vanilla, can also add sweetness to foods and drinks without the health risks associated with too much sugar. Incorporating these practices—choosing whole grains rich in fiber, eating a rainbow of fruits and vegetables, and cutting back on refined sugars—puts you on the path to a healthier, more balanced life. These carbohydrate choices support the DASH diet's principles, align with heart health goals, and provide the fuel your body needs in the most nutrient-rich forms. Embrace these elements, and watch as they transform not just your meals but also your overall well-being.

3. PROTEINS AND FATS

In the colorful world of healthy eating, proteins and fats play starring roles, each bringing unique and essential benefits to our tables and bodies. While proteins are the building blocks, giving structure and strength to every cell, fats serve as both a rich source of energy and vital players in maintaining healthy cells and brains. Understanding how to select and balance these vital nutrients can transform your approach to food, aligning beautifully with a heart-healthy, DASH-oriented lifestyle.

Lean Protein Sources

When you think of protein, you might imagine a big, juicy steak, but there are many other heart-friendly ways to meet your protein needs. Lean proteins provide the necessary amino acids for muscle repair and immune function without excessive saturated fat, making them a smarter choice for cardiovascular health.

Chicken and turkey breast top the list as popular lean meats, but don't overlook plant-based sources like lentils, beans, chickpeas, and tofu. These vegetarian options are not only rich in protein but also bring fiber and various minerals to your plate, promoting digestive health and increasing satiety.

Fish, particularly fatty varieties like salmon, mackerel, and sardines, are double-duty foods. They are excellent sources of protein and omega-3 fatty acids, which are known for their heart-protective properties. Including fish in your meals a couple of times a week can support heart health by reducing inflammation and decreasing the risk of heart disease.

Healthy Fats and Their Benefits

Gone are the days when all fats were branded as bad. Today, we understand the importance of healthy fats in diet, particularly those rich in omega-3 and omega-6 fatty acids, which are crucial for brain health and can help manage cholesterol levels.

Monounsaturated and polyunsaturated fats, found in olive oil, avocados, nuts, and seeds, are not just good for you—they're essential. They help absorb vitamins and protect your heart by maintaining levels of good HDL cholesterol while reducing harmful LDL cholesterol.

Think of adding these fats not just as a nutritional necessity but as an opportunity to enhance the flavor of your meals. Drizzling olive oil over a salad or swirling some avocado into a smoothie can elevate your dishes, making them tastier and more satisfying.

Avoiding Trans Fats and Processed Meats

While embracing healthy fats, it's equally important to avoid their unhealthy counterparts. Trans fats, for example, are found in many fried foods, baked goods, and packaged snacks. These fats contribute to heart disease by increasing harmful LDL cholesterol and reducing beneficial HDL cholesterol. They're sneaky enemies of heart health, often hiding in plain sight on ingredient lists as "partially hydrogenated oils."

Similarly, processed meats like sausages, bacon, and deli meats often contain high levels of sodium and preservatives, which can raise blood pressure and increase the risk of heart disease. These meats can be particularly pernicious due to their convenience and prevalence in fast foods and easy grab-and-go meals.

Instead, opt for fresh or frozen meats without added sauces or flavorings and use natural herbs and spices to enhance their flavor. When it comes to fats, choose whole food sources and be vigilant about reading food labels to steer clear of trans fats, opting instead for healthier fats that support your well-being.

Navigating the world of proteins and fats on the DASH diet does not have to be complicated. By choosing lean proteins, embracing healthy fats, and avoiding harmful ones, you can enjoy delicious, nutritious meals that support not only your heart health but your overall vitality. With each mindful choice, remember you're not just feeding yourself; you're nurturing your heart, brain, and body on the most fundamental levels, creating a stronger, happier you.

CHAPTER 5: COMPLEMENTARY HEALTHY HABITS

Embarking on the DASH diet is much like planting a garden—it's not just about the seeds you sow, but also about nurturing them with water, sunlight, and careful attention. Similarly, while following the DASH diet principles is the seed of your wellness garden, a trio of overlooked yet crucial elements—hydration, stress management, and sleep—acts as the sustaining sunlight, water, and soil, ensuring your health blossoms beautifully.

Hydration, often as simple as drinking enough water, is akin to the quiet nurturer of your body's garden. It's surprisingly easy to overlook, yet it's essential for transporting nutrients, keeping joints lubricated, and aiding in digestion. Imagine water as the carrier of life within you, touching every aspect of your health quietly yet powerfully.

Then, consider the role of stress management—it's not just a buzzword, but a vital part of your health regimen. The modern world buzzes with stressors, akin to weeds threatening to choke the vibrant life out of your garden. Crafting peaceful moments within your day, be it through meditation, a relaxing walk, or a joyful stretch, can significantly bolster your bodily systems, aligning perfectly with the DASH diet's health goals.

Lastly, sleep, the silent healer, sweeps in like the cool, soothing night after a sunny day. It recalibrates the body, repairs tissues, and resets your heart rate, interspersing your efforts with the rest it needs to thrive. Just as a garden rests under the moonlight, preparing for the next day's growth burst, your body uses sleep to prepare for another day of flourishing health.

Together, these practices create a robust framework, supporting your journey on the DASH diet. They aren't just complementary habits but essential components that facilitate the full flowering of your health. As we walk through each of these elements, remember that incorporating them into your daily routine isn't just about adhering to a diet. It's about crafting a lifestyle that fosters vitality, resilience, and happiness in your life's vibrant garden.

---

1. Hydration and Its Importance

Water is as essential to our body's health and wellness as sunlight is to the green leaves of a plant. Sometimes, the simplest habits we can adopt to improve our health are the most profound, and maintaining proper hydration is a testament to this truth. As someone following the DASH diet, realizing the role water plays in your daily health routine is crucial. It's not merely about quenching thirst; it's about setting a foundation for a life of vitality.

Imagine your body as a complex network of rivers and streams. Each cell, each organ functions optimally when there is effective water flow. When the water diminishes, just like a riverbed during drought, our bodies begin to show signs of strain. Here, hydration does not only support our physical well-being but also our mental sharpness and emotional balance.

How Much Water Do You Need?

Determining how much water you need isn't a one-size-fits-all answer. It can change with lifestyle, health conditions, and even the climate you live in. However, a general rule has often been to aim for eight 8-ounce glasses, which equals about 2 liters, or half a gallon a day. This is the 8×8 rule and is easy to remember.

Yet, individual water needs can vary. Factors such as exercise, environmental conditions, overall health, and whether you're pregnant or breastfeeding play crucial roles in your body's hydration needs. For instance, if you engage in any activity that makes you sweat, you need to drink extra water to cover the fluid loss. It's crucial to hydrate before, during, and after a workout. Also, environments that are hot or humid will result in higher fluid loss, as will periods of illness with symptoms like fever or vomiting.

For those on the DASH diet, it's also worth noting that as you increase your intake of fruits and vegetables, which are high in water content, you might not need as much additional water. But remember, the goal is consistent, adequate hydration, so listen to your body's signals.

Benefits of Staying Hydrated

Hydration is not just about warding off the feeling of thirst. Its benefits ripple across multiple facets of our health.

1. **Enhanced Physical Performance**: Adequate hydration contributes to optimal physical performance. Underhydration can lead to reduced motivation, increased fatigue, and makes exercise feel much more laborious, both physically and mentally.
2. **Efficient Digestion and Weight Management**: Water is a crucial player in the process of digestion. It aids in breaking down food and absorbing nutrients effectively. Drinking water before meals can also make you feel fuller; thus, it might help prevent overeating.
3. **Detoxification**: Our body's built-in detox system—liver, kidneys, gastrointestinal tract, skin, and lungs—depends on water to flush out waste products.
4. **Healthier Skin**: Staying hydrated helps to keep your skin supple and resilient. While it won't necessarily ward off wrinkles, it's vital for maintaining optimal skin moisture and delivering essential nutrients to the skin cells.
5. **Cognitive Function and Mood Improvement**: Several studies suggest that even mild dehydration can impair brain function, memory, and mood in all age groups.

Being in touch with your body's needs and recognizing the early signs of dehydration, such as dry mouth, tiredness, or decreased urine output, can help you maintain water balance before noticeable dehydration sets in.

Infused Water Recipes

One delightful way to ensure you meet your hydration goals is by preparing infused water. It adds a pleasant twist to plain water and can make your hydration routine more enjoyable. Here are a few simple recipes to enrich your water with flavor and health benefits:

- **Citrus Burst**: Slice one orange, one lime, and one lemon into thin slices. Combine in a pitcher with water and refrigerate for at least an hour. This mix not only invigorates the water with a refreshing citrus flavor but also infuses it with Vitamin C.
- **Ginger Mint**: Slice a two-inch piece of fresh ginger and add it to a pitcher of water with a handful of fresh mint leaves. This infusion can aid digestion and adds a spicy kick to your palate.
- **Cucumber Basil**: Thinly slice one cucumber and add it to a pitcher of water along with a few fresh basil leaves. This combination is wonderfully refreshing and perfect for a hot day.

These infused water recipes not only make the water appealing but also provide a subtle introduction of vitamins and antioxidants into your diet. Plus, they can serve as a beautiful centerpiece on your dining or kitchen table, subtly reminding you and your family to drink more water throughout the day.

Remember, keeping hydrated is more than just a pillar of physical health; it's a foundational habit that supports your mental clarity, emotional well-being, and overall lifestyle goals. It's not just about following a rule but about learning and listening to what your body needs, a true harmony between your body's needs and your daily practices. So, as you continue to unfold the benefits of the DASH diet, think of water as your partner, silently amplifying your efforts and supporting your journey towards a healthier life.

2. STRESS MANAGEMENT TECHNIQUES

In our fast-paced world, the buzz of alarms, the ping of smartphone notifications, and the constant juggle of home and work responsibilities can make even the calmest days feel chaotic. Learning to manage this stress is not merely a luxury, but a necessity for maintaining both mental and physical health, especially when adhering to lifestyle changes such as the DASH diet. Stress management is a crucial partner in your journey toward health, subtly weaving itself into your daily routines and making significant differences in your overall well-being.

Relaxation and Mindfulness

Imagine for a moment the tranquil silence of a morning just before sunrise, or the peaceful solitude of the world as it winds down at dusk. These moments hold a quality of peace that many of us long for in our daily lives. Mindfulness and relaxation techniques are ways to capture this tranquility and weave it into the tapestry of our everyday lives.

Mindfulness refers to the practice of being present and fully engaged with whatever we're doing at the moment — free from distraction or judgment, and aware of our thoughts and feelings without getting caught up in them. It allows us to awake to the fullness of each moment. Daily practice can help reduce stress and anxiety, improve attention, and enhance the feeling of emotional well-being.

Begin with simple breathing exercises, which you can do at any point in your day. Sit or lie down in a quiet place, close your eyes, and take a deep breath, focusing fully on the sensation of the air moving in and out of your lungs. This simple act can serve as a 'reset button' for your nervous system.

Progressing from breathing exercises, guided meditation apps or classes can also be beneficial. These resources provide structured mindfulness exercises and can be particularly useful for beginners who may appreciate the guiding voice of an instructor.

Physical Activity and Stress Reduction

Incorporating regular physical activity into your routine isn't just about keeping your heart healthy and maintaining a weight that's right for your body. Exercise also plays an essential role in stress management. When you engage in physical activity, your body releases endorphins, chemicals in the brain that act as natural painkillers and mood elevators. Consider, for example, how a brisk walk in the fresh air can change your perspective on a stressful day, or how a yoga session can relax both your mind and body.

The key to using exercise as a stress management tool is to choose activities that you enjoy and can perform regularly without feeling burdened. If you love dancing, put on some music and dance around your living room. If you enjoy quiet, solitary activities, consider cycling, jogging, or walking in a natural setting. Regularity is more beneficial than intensity for stress reduction.

Creating a Balanced Lifestyle

Balancing the many aspects of life—work, family, social obligations, and self-care—can often feel like an art form that's difficult to master. However, creating a lifestyle that allows for these elements to coexist harmoniously is critical for stress management. It's about setting limits and boundaries that respect your physical, emotional, and mental well-being.

Start by examining your routine. Are there activities consuming disproportionate amounts of your time and energy? Are you spending enough time on activities that nourish you not just physically but also mentally and emotionally? Sometimes, simplifying your schedule is all it takes to create a more balanced lifestyle. This might mean learning to say no to extra tasks at work, or choosing to spend time at home rather than committing to social events that leave you drained rather than energized.

Time management strategies, such as prioritizing tasks, breaking large projects into manageable steps, and using a planner can also help alleviate stress. These methods allow you to clear mental clutter by externalizing what you need to remember and when you need to do it, which reduces anxiety.

Creating a bedtime routine that allows you to wind down and get enough sleep is another essential part of maintaining balance. Avoid stimulants like caffeine and electronic devices in the hours leading up to bed, and try to go to sleep and wake up at the same time every day. This regularity can improve both the quality of your sleep and your body's ability to manage stress.

Practicing stress management through mindfulness, physical activity, and lifestyle balance doesn't just help preserve your health — it enhances your ability to enjoy life. Each individual's stressors are unique and so too should be their coping strategies. Tailor these techniques to fit your individual life circumstances and watch as life's trials become a little less stressful and a lot more manageable, perfectly complementing the principles of the DASH diet. With stress under control, everything from your mood to your heart health can improve, opening the door to a fuller, more vibrant life.

---

3. Sleep and Recovery

Imagine the silence of the world at night, a time for rest and recovery, not just for our bustling cities but for our bodies and minds as well. Sleep, often underrated, plays a crucial role in our well-being, akin to that of diet and exercise. It's during these quiet hours that our body repairs itself, consolidates memories, and rejuvenates for the next day. In the context of the DASH diet and overall cardiovascular health, sleep becomes an even more essential pillar of maintaining balance and health.

Importance of Quality Sleep

Quality sleep does much more than just prevent you from feeling groggy. It affects various aspects of your health, from brain function and emotional well-being to cardiovascular health and metabolic processes. During sleep, your body undertakes the critical task of repairing heart and blood vessels. It is also a key time for the brain to process and consolidate the experiences and information from the day into long-term memory and learning.

Studies have shown that inadequate sleep can trigger a stress response in the body, increasing the production of stress hormones, which can raise blood pressure and heart rate. These are the very conditions that the DASH diet seeks to mitigate. Thus, enhancing sleep quality is not just complementary to dietary efforts but is integral to achieving the best health outcomes.

Tips for Better Sleep Hygiene

Improving sleep can sometimes feel like a daunting task, especially if you've spent years with erratic sleep schedules or poor bedtime routines. However, implementing effective sleep hygiene can profoundly impact your sleep quality and, by extension, your overall health.

1. **Consistency is Key**: Go to bed and wake up at the same time every day, including weekends. This regularity helps to regulate your body's internal clock and could help you fall asleep and wake up more naturally.
2. **Create a Restful Environment**: Keep your bedroom cool, quiet, and dark. Invest in good quality bedding and use shades or curtains to block out light. Consider using earplugs or white noise machines to drown out disruptive sounds.
3. **Wind Down Routinely**: Develop a pre-sleep routine that signals to your body it's time to wind down. This might include reading a book, taking a warm bath, or doing gentle stretches. Avoid stimulating activities like checking emails or engaging with intense media.
4. **Watch What You Consume**: Avoid large meals, caffeine, and alcohol before bedtime as they can disrupt sleep. If you have trouble abandoning evening snacks, opt for something light and healthy.
5. **Limit Screen Time**: The blue light emitted by your phone, tablet, computer, or TV can interfere with your ability to fall asleep. Try to turn off these devices at least an hour before bedtime.
6. **Exercise Regularly**: But do it earlier in the day. Morning or afternoon workouts can help regulate your sleep pattern. However, vigorous exercise too close to bedtime might increase adrenaline levels and make it harder to fall asleep.

Incorporating these habits into your daily routine doesn't have to be an overhaul overnight. Start small, perhaps by adjusting your bedtime or creating a relaxing pre-sleep routine, and gradually build upon these changes as they become ingrained in your nightly habit.

Impact of Sleep on Overall Health

The effects of sleep extend beyond mere cognitive and physical health; it's a cornerstone of emotional well-being. Lack of sleep has been linked to irritability and stress, while good sleep can enhance mood, make you more patient, and increase your ability to concentrate and react quickly.

Moreover, sleep has a profound impact on the metabolic processes related to blood sugar and the regulation of hormones affecting your appetite. Studies suggest that poor sleep patterns are linked to higher risks of various health problems, including cardiovascular disease, diabetes, and obesity—the very disorders that the DASH diet helps manage.

For those following the DASH diet, understanding the symbiotic relationship between diet and sleep can enhance your ability to maintain not only a healthy blood pressure but overall vitality. When your body has had enough rest, you're better equipped to make thoughtful food choices and have the energy for physical activity. Remember, achieving good sleep is a journey, one that mirrors the principles of the DASH diet: balanced, consistent, and integral to your long-term health. By prioritizing sleep, you not only boost your immediate energy but also support your body's ability to thrive in the long term, making each day brighter, more productive, and healthful. As you continue to nurture your body with good nutrition and moderate exercise, let sleep be the time when all your healthy choices come together to rejuvenate and empower you for another day.

CHAPTER 6: BREAKFAST RECIPES

Good morning! Whether you're someone who wakes up ready to take on the day or someone who hits the snooze button more than once, breakfast is your foundational start. For many of us, breakfast is a rushed cup of coffee and possibly a slice of toast squeezed in before the day's commitments sweep us away. However, with the DASH diet, we aim to transform this meal into a valuable opportunity for nourishing your body right from the start, while still honoring that ever-pressing need for convenience.

Imagine sitting down to a meal that feels more like a treat than a routine, yet sets you up with balanced nutrition that fuels your busy day. It's not just possible; it's easy with the recipes we've curated for you in this chapter. From the warming comfort of oatmeal, invigorated with a dash of cinnamon and a swirl of fresh fruits, to innovative smoothie bowls that you can whip up in less than five minutes—these are breakfasts designed to make you look forward to mornings!

With each recipe, I've kept in mind that while your schedule may be packed, your meals can still be satisfying and aligned with the DASH diet principles. Picture this: you, bustling around the kitchen, as a delicious and heart-healthy breakfast comes together in no time. You leave your house not just on time, but empowered, knowing you've given your body what it needs to thrive.

These breakfast recipes are more than just food; they are your first victory of the day. They prove that a nutritious, delicious breakfast doesn't require an unrealistic slice of your morning. Each dish has been thoughtfully designed to balance ease with health and flavor with speed, ensuring that no matter how hurried your mornings are, you can still begin with a meal that's both satisfying and good for you.

So, flip these pages and let's start these mornings transformed, energized by tastes that excite and nourish. Welcome to breakfast on the DASH diet—where your day begins with a dash of health and a hefty portion of flavor!

---

1. QUICK AND EASY BREAKFASTS

CLASSIC BERRY ALMOND OVERNIGHT OATS

Preparation Time: 10 min.
Cooking Time: none
Mode of Cooking: No Cooking
Servings: 2

Ingredients:

- 1 C. old-fashioned oats
- 1 C. unsweetened almond milk
- ½ C. Greek yogurt, plain
- 1 Tbsp chia seeds
- 1 Tbsp honey
- ½ C. mixed berries (blueberries, raspberries)
- 2 Tbsp slivered almonds

Directions:

1. Combine oats, almond milk, Greek yogurt, chia seeds, and honey in a bowl; stir well
2. Divide the mixture between two jars
3. Top each with mixed berries and slivered almonds
4. Seal and refrigerate overnight

Tips:

- Try using frozen berries for a cost-effective option
- Add a sprinkle of cinnamon for a flavor boost
- Swap honey for maple syrup if preferred

Nutritional Values: Calories: 325, Fat: 9g, Carbs: 49g, Protein: 15g, Sugar: 12g, Sodium: 55 mg, Potassium: 336 mg, Cholesterol: 5 mg

PEANUT BUTTER BANANA OVERNIGHT OATS

Preparation Time: 10 min.
Cooking Time: none
Mode of Cooking: No Cooking
Servings: 2
Ingredients:

- 1 C. rolled oats
- 1 C. low-fat milk
- ½ C. Greek yogurt, plain
- 1 Tbsp natural peanut butter
- 1 Tbsp ground flaxseed
- 1 ripe banana, mashed
- 1 tsp vanilla extract
- 1 Tbsp honey

Directions:

1. Mix oats, milk, Greek yogurt, peanut a butter, flaxseed, mashed banana, vanilla extract, and honey together in a large bowl
2. Stir thoroughly to combine
3. Spoon into jars and tightly seal
4. Refrigerate overnight

Tips:

- Experiment with adding a scoop of protein powder for an added nutrient boost
- Top with a small handful of granola for extra crunch before serving
- Use almond butter as a substitute for peanut butter if desired

Nutritional Values: Calories: 380, Fat: 10g, Carbs: 56g, Protein: 17g, Sugar: 20g, Sodium: 65 mg, Potassium: 545 mg, Cholesterol: 7 mg

TROPICAL COCONUT OVERNIGHT OATS

Preparation Time: 10 min.
Cooking Time: none
Mode of Cooking: No Cooking
Servings: 2
Ingredients:

- 1 C. steel-cut oats
- 1 C. coconut milk
- ½ C. Greek yogurt, vanilla flavor
- 1 Tbsp shredded coconut
- 1 Tbsp honey
- ½ C. pineapple chunks
- 1 kiwi, diced

Directions:

1. Combine steel-cut oats, coconut milk, Greek yogurt, shredded coconut, and honey in a mixing bowl
2. Mix well until all ingredients are evenly distributed
3. Add pineapple chunks and kiwi to the mixture
4. Pour into jars, seal, and refrigerate overnight

Tips:

- Use light coconut milk to reduce fat content
- Substitute pineapple and kiwi with mango and papaya for a different tropical twist
- Drizzle a little lime juice over the top for extra zing before serving

Nutritional Values: Calories: 310, Fat: 12g, Carbs: 44g, Protein: 9g, Sugar: 15g, Sodium: 40 mg, Potassium: 382 mg, Cholesterol: 3 mg

BERRY ALMOND SUNRISE BOWL

Preparation Time: 5 min.
Cooking Time: none
Mode of Cooking: No Cooking
Servings: 1

Ingredients:

- ½ C. rolled oats
- 1 C. almond milk
- ¼ C. Greek yogurt
- ½ banana, sliced
- ¼ C. blueberries
- ¼ C. raspberries
- 1 Tbsp chia seeds
- 1 Tbsp sliced almonds
- 1 Tbsp honey

Directions:

1. Combine rolled oats and almond milk in a bowl and let sit overnight
2. In the morning, add Greek yogurt and mix well
3. Top with banana slices, blueberries, raspberries, chia seeds, and sliced almonds
4. Drizzle with honey

Tips:

- Soak oats in the refrigerator for easier morning preparation
- Add a scoop of protein powder for an extra protein boost
- Substitute honey with agave syrup for a vegan option

Nutritional Values: Calories: 355, Fat: 9g, Carbs: 53g, Protein: 15g, Sugar: 18g, Sodium: 35 mg, Potassium: 475 mg, Cholesterol: 3 mg

GREEN TROPICAL ENERGY BOWL

Preparation Time: 7 min.
Cooking Time: none
Mode of Cooking: No Cooking
Servings: 1
Ingredients:

- 1 C. fresh spinach
- 1 kiwi, peeled and sliced
- ½ C. pineapple chunks
- ½ banana, sliced
- 1 C. coconut water
- 1 Tbsp flax seeds
- 1 Tbsp coconut flakes
- 1 tsp spirulina powder

Directions:

1. Blend spinach, kiwi, pineapple chunks, banana, and coconut water until smooth
2. Pour into a bowl
3. Garnish with flax seeds, coconut flakes, and a sprinkle of spirulina powder

Tips:

- Include a handful of ice in the blending process for a chilled effect
- Spirulina adds a boost of nutrients but can be omitted for a milder taste
- Increase the sweetness by adding a bit of honey if desired

Nutritional Values: Calories: 290, Fat: 5g, Carbs: 60g, Protein: 5g, Sugar: 35g, Sodium: 55 mg, Potassium: 850 mg, Cholesterol: 0 mg

PEANUT BUTTER BANANA BLISS BOWL

Preparation Time: 6 min.
Cooking Time: none
Mode of Cooking: No Cooking
Servings: 1
Ingredients:

- 1 frozen banana
- 2 Tbsp peanut butter
- ½ C. Greek yogurt
- ½ C. almond milk
- 1 Tbsp cocoa powder
- 1 Tbsp honey
- 1 Tbsp granola
- 1 tsp hemp seeds

Directions:

1. Blend frozen banana, peanut butter, Greek yogurt, almond milk, and cocoa powder until smooth and creamy
2. Pour mixture into a bowl

3. Top with granola, a drizzle of honey, and hemp seeds

Tips:

- Use natural peanut butter to keep it low in sodium and sugar
- Freeze the banana the night before for a creamier texture
- Swap honey with maple syrup for a different sweetness

Nutritional Values: Calories: 415, Fat: 16g, Carbs: 53g, Protein: 18g, Sugar: 27g, Sodium: 100 mg, Potassium: 600 mg, Cholesterol: 3 mg

CINNAMON SPICE WHOLE GRAIN PANCAKES

Preparation Time: 15 min.
Cooking Time: 10 min.
Mode of Cooking: Stove-Top
Servings: 4
Ingredients:

- 1 cup whole wheat flour
- ½ cup rolled oats
- 1 Tbsp baking powder
- ¼ tsp salt
- 1 tsp ground cinnamon
- ½ tsp nutmeg
- 2 Tbsp honey
- 1 large egg
- 1 cup low-fat milk
- 2 Tbsp olive oil
- 1 tsp vanilla extract

Directions:

1. Combine whole wheat flour, rolled oats, baking powder, salt, cinnamon, and nutmeg in a large bowl
2. In another bowl, whisk together honey, egg, milk, olive oil, and vanilla extract
3. Pour wet ingredients into dry ingredients and stir until just combined
4. Heat a non-stick skillet over medium heat and pour ¼ cup of batter for each pancake

5. Cook until bubbles form on the surface, then flip and cook until golden brown

Tips:

- Experiment with adding fresh or dried fruit to the batter for extra sweetness and nutrients
- Use a non-stick skillet or griddle to minimize the need for extra oil
- Serve with a drizzle of honey or pure maple syrup instead of processed syrups

Nutritional Values: Calories: 210, Fat: 8g, Carbs: 32g, Protein: 7g, Sugar: 8g, Sodium: 200 mg, Potassium: 155 mg, Cholesterol: 55 mg

BLUEBERRY LEMON WHOLE GRAIN PANCAKES

Preparation Time: 15 min.
Cooking Time: 10 min.
Mode of Cooking: Stove-Top
Servings: 4
Ingredients:

- 1 cup whole wheat flour
- ½ cup rolled oats
- 1 Tbsp baking powder
- ¼ tsp salt
- 1 Tbsp granulated Stevia
- 1 cup fresh blueberries
- Zest of 1 lemon
- 1 large egg
- 1¼ cups almond milk
- 1 Tbsp olive oil
- 1 tsp lemon extract

Directions:

1. Mix whole wheat flour, rolled oats, baking powder, salt, and Stevia in a large mixing bowl
2. In a separate bowl, beat egg with almond milk, olive oil, and lemon extract
3. Stir wet ingredients into dry until combined, then fold in blueberries and lemon zest
4. Heat a non-stick pan over medium heat, scoop ¼ cup of batter per pancake, cook until bubbles appear then flip until done

Tips:
- Add lemon zest right before cooking to enhance the lemon flavor
- If available, use wild blueberries for a burst of antioxidant power
- To keep pancakes warm while cooking batches, set them in an oven preheated to 200°F (93°C)

Nutritional Values: Calories: 180, Fat: 5g, Carbs: 30g, Protein: 6g, Sugar: 5g, Sodium: 220 mg, Potassium: 125 mg, Cholesterol: 53 mg

APPLE CINNAMON OATMEAL PANCAKES

Preparation Time: 20 min.
Cooking Time: 15 min.
Mode of Cooking: Stove-Top
Servings: 6
Ingredients:

- 1½ cups whole wheat flour
- 1 cup oatmeal
- 1 Tbsp baking powder
- ½ tsp salt
- 2 Tbsp brown sugar
- 1 tsp cinnamon
- 2 large eggs
- 1½ cups skim milk
- 1 apple, peeled and grated
- 2 Tbsp unsalted butter, melted
- 1 tsp vanilla extract

Directions:

1. Whisk together whole wheat flour, oatmeal, baking powder, salt, brown sugar, and cinnamon in a bowl
2. In a separate bowl, mix eggs, skim milk, grated apple, melted butter, and vanilla extract
3. Combine wet and dry ingredients and stir until smooth
4. Heat a non-stick skillet over medium heat, pour ⅓ cup of batter for each pancake, cook until golden on both sides

Tips:
- Incorporate grated apple in the batter for natural sweetness and moisture
- Serve these pancakes with a dollop of low-fat yogurt and a sprinkle of chopped nuts for extra protein
- Keep pancakes small to ensure they cook thoroughly and evenly

Nutritional Values: Calories: 230, Fat: 7g, Carbs: 35g, Protein: 8g, Sugar: 10g, Sodium: 210 mg, Potassium: 180 mg, Cholesterol: 63 mg

2. HEARTY AND SAVORY OPTIONS

SPINACH AND MUSHROOM FRITTATA

Preparation Time: 15 min
Cooking Time: 25 min
Mode of Cooking: Baking
Servings: 6
Ingredients:

- 8 large eggs
- 1 cup fresh spinach, chopped
- 1/2 cup mushrooms, sliced
- 1/4 cup onions, finely chopped
- 2 cloves garlic, minced
- 1/4 cup low-fat milk
- 1/2 cup feta cheese, crumbled
- 1 Tbsp olive oil
- Salt to taste
- Black pepper to taste

Directions:

1. Preheat oven to 375°F (190°C)
2. In a skillet, heat olive oil over medium heat and sauté onions and garlic until translucent
3. Add mushrooms and cook until softened
4. Stir in spinach and cook until wilted
5. In a bowl, whisk together eggs, milk, salt, and pepper
6. Add cooked vegetables to the egg mixture, then stir in feta cheese

7. Pour into a greased 9-inch pie dish and bake for 25 minutes or until the eggs are set and the top is lightly golden

Tips:

- Try adding a pinch of nutmeg for a depth of flavor
- Serve with a side of fresh tomato salsa for added freshness

Nutritional Values: Calories: 180, Fat: 12g, Carbs: 3g, Protein: 16g, Sugar: 2g, Sodium: 200 mg, Potassium: 240 mg, Cholesterol: 370 mg

BELL PEPPER AND POTATO FRITTATA

Preparation Time: 20 min
Cooking Time: 30 min
Mode of Cooking: Baking
Servings: 4
Ingredients:

- 4 large eggs
- 1 large bell pepper, diced
- 1 small potato, peeled and diced
- 1/4 cup red onion, diced
- 1 Tbsp olive oil
- 1/4 tsp smoked paprika
- 1/4 cup grated parmesan cheese
- Salt to taste
- Black pepper to taste

Directions:

1. Preheat oven to 375°F (190°C)
2. In a non-stick skillet, heat olive oil and sauté bell peppers, potato, and onion until soft, about 7-10 minutes
3. Season with smoked paprika, salt, and pepper
4. In a bowl, whisk eggs with parmesan cheese and a pinch of salt and pepper
5. Add sautéed vegetables to the egg mixture and mix well
6. Pour into a baking dish and bake for about 30 minutes or until set and golden brown

Tips:

- Add a sprinkle of chili flakes for a spicy kick
- Pair with a fresh green salad

Nutritional Values: Calories: 220, Fat: 15g, Carbs: 12g, Protein: 12g, Sugar: 2g, Sodium: 180 mg, Potassium: 350 mg, Cholesterol: 220 mg

ASPARAGUS AND GOAT CHEESE FRITTATA

Preparation Time: 10 min
Cooking Time: 20 min
Mode of Cooking: Baking
Servings: 4
Ingredients:

- 6 eggs
- 1 cup asparagus, chopped
- 1/4 cup scallions, sliced
- 1/2 cup goat cheese, crumbled
- 1 Tbsp olive oil
- Salt to taste
- Black pepper to taste

Directions:

1. Preheat oven to 375°F (190°C)
2. Briefly blanch asparagus in boiling water, then drain and set aside
3. Heat olive oil in a skillet and sauté scallions until tender
4. Beat eggs with salt and pepper in a bowl
5. Stir in asparagus, scallions, and crumbled goat cheese
6. Pour mixture into a greased baking pan and bake for 20 minutes or until eggs are set and top is slightly golden

Tips:

- Serve with a drizzle of balsamic reduction for an elegant finish
- Good with toasted multigrain bread

Nutritional Values: Calories: 200, Fat: 15g, Carbs: 5g, Protein: 13g, Sugar: 3g, Sodium: 190 mg, Potassium: 180 mg, Cholesterol: 330 mg

Spicy Avocado Toast with Egg

Preparation Time: 5 min
Cooking Time: 6 min
Mode of Cooking: Toasting, Frying
Servings: 1
Ingredients:

- 1 slice whole grain bread
- 1 ripe avocado
- 1 large egg
- 1/8 tsp chili flakes
- 1/4 tsp lime juice
- Salt and pepper to taste
- 1 Tbsp olive oil

Directions:

1. Toast bread until golden
2. In a bowl, mash avocado with lime juice, chili flakes, salt, and pepper
3. Spread avocado mixture on toasted bread
4. In a skillet, heat olive oil over medium heat and fry the egg until desired doneness
5. Place fried egg on top of avocado toast

Tips:

- Add a pinch of crushed garlic to avocado mixture for extra zing
- Experiment with different types of bread for variety

Nutritional Values: Calories: 290, Fat: 21g, Carbs: 24g, Protein: 10g, Sugar: 3g, Sodium: 320mg, Potassium: 650mg, Cholesterol: 185mg

Mediterranean Avocado Toast

Preparation Time: 8 min
Cooking Time: none
Mode of Cooking: No Cooking
Servings: 1
Ingredients:

- 1 slice sourdough bread
- 1 ripe avocado
- 2 Tbsp feta cheese, crumbled
- 5 cherry tomatoes, halved
- 1 Tbsp chopped red onion
- 1 Tbsp olives, sliced
- 1 tsp olive oil
- 1/4 tsp oregano

Directions:

1. Toast sourdough bread until crisp
2. Mash avocado and spread on toast
3. Top with crumbled feta cheese, cherry tomatoes, red onion, and olives
4. Drizzle with olive oil and sprinkle oregano on top

Tips:

- To enhance flavors, let the toppings marinate together for about 10 min before assembling
- Optionally, add a few leaves of fresh basil for a fresh flavor boost

Nutritional Values: Calories: 320, Fat: 20g, Carbs: 29g, Protein: 7g, Sugar: 4g, Sodium: 510mg, Potassium: 487mg, Cholesterol: 15mg

Smoked Salmon Avocado Toast

Preparation Time: 7 min
Cooking Time: none
Mode of Cooking: No Cooking
Servings: 1
Ingredients:

- 1 slice rye bread
- 1 ripe avocado
- 2 oz smoked salmon
- 1 Tbsp cream cheese
- 1 Tbsp capers
- 1 tsp lemon juice
- Fresh dill for garnish
- Salt and black pepper to taste

Directions:

1. Toast rye bread until crunchy
2. Mix avocado with lemon juice, salt, and pepper and spread on the toast

3. Layer smoked salmon over the avocado
4. Add dollops of cream cheese and sprinkle capers and dill on top

Tips:

- Using low-fat cream cheese reduces overall fat content
- Lemon zest can be added for an extra citrus kick

Nutritional Values: Calories: 400, Fat: 27g, Carbs: 29g, Protein: 18g, Sugar: 4g, Sodium: 670mg, Potatoes: 559mg, Cholesterol: 30mg

SUNRISE BERRY & GRANOLA GREEK YOGURT PARFAIT

Preparation Time: 10 min
Cooking Time: none
Mode of Cooking: No Cooking
Servings: 2
Ingredients:

- 2 cups plain Greek yogurt
- 1 cup mixed berries (blueberries, strawberries, raspberries)
- ½ cup low-fat granola
- 1 Tbsp honey
- 2 tsp chia seeds

Directions:

1. Layer half of the Greek yogurt in two glasses
2. Add a layer of mixed berries
3. Sprinkle granola over the berries
4. Drizzle honey and sprinkle chia seeds
5. Repeat the layering with the remaining ingredients

Tips:

- Serve immediately or refrigerate overnight for a thicker texture
- Adjust the amount of honey based on your sweetness preference
- Mix in a few drops of vanilla extract to yogurt for enhanced flavor

Nutritional Values: Calories: 290, Fat: 4g, Carbs: 42g, Protein: 20g, Sugar: 26g, Sodium: 60 mg, Potassium: 300 mg, Cholesterol: 10 mg

TROPICAL COCONUT GREEK YOGURT PARFAIT

Preparation Time: 15 min
Cooking Time: none
Mode of Cooking: No Cooking
Servings: 2
Ingredients:

- 2 cups plain Greek yogurt
- 1 cup diced mango
- ½ cup pineapple chunks
- ½ cup low-fat granola
- ¼ cup coconut flakes, unsweetened
- 1 Tbsp honey

Directions:

1. Layer half of the Greek yogurt into two bowls
2. Add a layer of mango and pineapple chunks
3. Sprinkle granola and coconut flakes
4. Drizzle with honey
5. Repeat the layers with the remaining ingredients

Tips:

- Consider toasting the coconut flakes for an extra crunch
- Use agave syrup as an alternative sweetener if desired
- Chill before serving to allow the flavors to meld

Nutritional Values: Calories: 325, Fat: 5g, Carbs: 53g, Protein: 21g, Sugar: 38g, Sodium: 85 mg, Potassium: 500 mg, Cholesterol: 15 mg

POMEGRANATE AND PISTACHIO GREEK YOGURT PARFAIT

Preparation Time: 12 min
Cooking Time: none
Mode of Cooking: No Cooking
Servings: 2

Ingredients:

- 2 cups plain Greek yogurt
- 1 cup pomegranate seeds
- ½ cup shelled pistachios, roughly chopped
- ½ cup rolled oats
- 2 Tbsp honey
- 1 tsp ground cardamom

Directions:

1. Layer half of the Greek yogurt in two serving dishes
2. Add a layer of pomegranate seeds
3. Mix rolled oats with chopped pistachios and cardamom, sprinkle over the seeds
4. Drizzle honey
5. Repeat the layers with the remaining ingredients

Tips:

- Sprinkle a pinch of cardamom on top before serving for added aroma
- Prepare this parfait the night before to soften the oats slightly
- Use maple syrup as a honey alternative for a different sweetness profile

Nutritional Values: Calories: 315, Fat: 9g, Carbs: 41g, Protein: 22g, Sugar: 28g, Sodium: 70 mg, Potassium: 470 mg, Cholesterol: 15 mg

3. BREAKFASTS ON THE GO

SPINACH AND FETA BREAKFAST BURRITOS

Preparation Time: 15 min.
Cooking Time: 10 min.
Mode of Cooking: Pan-frying
Servings: 4
Ingredients:

- 4 whole wheat tortillas
- 1 cup fresh spinach, chopped
- 4 large eggs, lightly beaten
- ½ cup feta cheese, crumbled
- ¼ cup red onion, finely diced
- ½ tsp garlic powder
- ¼ tsp black pepper
- 1 Tbsp olive oil

Directions:

1. Heat the olive oil in a skillet over medium heat
2. Add red onion and sauté until translucent
3. Add spinach and cook until wilted
4. Pour in beaten eggs, garlic powder, and black pepper, scrambling until eggs are set
5. Remove from heat and mix in feta cheese
6. Divide the mixture among the tortillas, roll them up tightly, and serve warm or wrap for on-the-go

Tips:

- Wrap burritos in foil to keep them warm for longer
- Add a dash of hot sauce for an extra kick
- Use egg whites only for a lower cholesterol option

Nutritional Values: Calories: 290, Fat: 15g, Carbs: 24g, Protein: 17g, Sugar: 3g, Sodium: 400 mg, Potassium: 200 mg, Cholesterol: 186 mg

TURKEY AND AVOCADO RANCH BURRITOS

Preparation Time: 20 min.
Cooking Time: 5 min.
Mode of Cooking: Pan-frying
Servings: 4
Ingredients:

- 4 whole wheat tortillas
- 1 cup cooked turkey breast, shredded
- 1 ripe avocado, sliced
- ½ cup cherry tomatoes, halved
- ¼ cup low-fat ranch dressing
- ¼ tsp cayenne pepper
- 1 Tbsp cilantro, chopped
- 1 Tbsp olive oil

Directions:

1. Heat olive oil in a skillet over medium-high heat
2. Add turkey and cayenne pepper, cook until slightly crispy
3. Remove from heat and combine turkey with ranch dressing and cilantro in a bowl
4. Place turkey mixture, avocado slices, and cherry tomatoes on each tortilla, roll up tightly, and serve or wrap for transport

Tips:

- Prep the ingredients the night before for quicker assembly in the morning
- Choose low-sodium turkey to maintain a healthier profile
- Swap ranch dressing for Greek yogurt mixed with herbs for a healthier option

Nutritional Values: Calories: 325, Fat: 15g, Carbs: 27g, Protein: 20g, Sugar: 2g, Sodium: 310 mg, Potassium: 450 mg, Cholesterol: 30 mg

MUSHROOM AND BELL PEPPER BREAKFAST BURRITOS

Preparation Time: 20 min.
Cooking Time: 15 min.
Mode of Cooking: Sautéing
Servings: 4
Ingredients:

- 4 whole wheat tortillas
- 1 cup bell peppers, sliced
- 1 cup mushrooms, sliced
- 4 large eggs, beaten
- 1/2 tsp chili flakes
- 1/4 tsp salt
- 1/4 cup cheddar cheese, shredded
- 1 Tbsp canola oil

Directions:

1. Heat canola oil in a large skillet over medium heat
2. Add bell peppers and mushrooms, sauté until soft
3. Add eggs, chili flakes, and salt, scramble until eggs are fully cooked
4. Stir in cheddar cheese until melted
5. Divide the egg mixture among the tortillas, roll up and serve immediately or wrap for later

Tips:

- Use a variety of colored bell peppers for a visually appealing meal
- Cook mushrooms until golden for deeper flavor
- Opt for low-fat cheese to reduce overall fat content

Nutritional Values: Calories: 275, Fat: 14g, Carbs: 22g, Protein: 18g, Sugar: 4g, Sodium: 340 mg, Potassium: 210 mg, Cholesterol: 215 mg

SPINACH AND FETA MUFFIN TIN OMELETS

Preparation Time: 15 min
Cooking Time: 20 min
Mode of Cooking: Baking
Servings: 6
Ingredients:

- 4 large eggs
- 1 cup fresh spinach, chopped
- 1/2 cup feta cheese, crumbled
- 1/4 cup red bell pepper, diced
- 1/4 cup onions, diced
- 1/2 tsp garlic powder
- 1/4 tsp black pepper
- Olive oil spray for greasing

Directions:

1. Preheat oven to 375°F (190°C)
2. Grease muffin tin cups with olive oil spray
3. In a bowl, whisk together eggs, garlic powder, and black pepper
4. Stir in spinach, feta, bell pepper, and onions
5. Evenly distribute the mixture into the muffin cups

6. Bake for 20 min or until eggs are set

Tips:

- Use silicone muffin cups for easier removal and cleaning
- Incorporate different veggies like mushrooms or zucchini for variety
- Serve with a dollop of low-fat Greek yogurt for extra creaminess

Nutritional Values: Calories: 110, Fat: 7g, Carbs: 3g, Protein: 9g, Sugar: 1g, Sodium: 200 mg, Potassium: 150 mg, Cholesterol: 185 mg

MUSHROOM AND SWISS MUFFIN TIN OMELETS

Preparation Time: 10 min
Cooking Time: 18 min
Mode of Cooking: Baking
Servings: 6
Ingredients:

- 4 large eggs
- 3/4 cup mushrooms, thinly sliced
- 1/2 cup Swiss cheese, shredded
- 1/4 cup green onions, chopped
- 1/2 tsp dried thyme
- Salt and pepper to taste
- Olive oil spray for greasing

Directions:

1. Preheat oven to 375°F (190°C)
2. Grease muffin tin cups with olive oil spray
3. In a bowl, whisk together eggs, thyme, salt, and pepper
4. Sauté mushrooms and green onions until tender and let cool slightly
5. Mix mushrooms, onions, and Swiss cheese into the egg mixture
6. Scoop into muffin cups and bake for 18 min

Tips:

- Avoid overfilling cups to prevent spillage during baking
- Feel free to swap Swiss cheese with another low-sodium cheese like mozzarella

- Pair with a side of fresh fruit for a balanced breakfast

Nutritional Values: Calories: 120, Fat: 8g, Carbs: 2g, Protein: 10g, Sugar: 1g, Sodium: 180 mg, Potassium: 125 mg, Cholesterol: 190 mg

TURKEY AND SPINACH MUFFIN TIN OMELETS

Preparation Time: 10 min
Cooking Time: 20 min
Mode of Cooking: Baking
Servings: 6
Ingredients:

- 4 large eggs
- 3/4 cup cooked turkey breast, chopped
- 1 cup spinach, finely chopped
- 1/2 cup low-fat cheddar cheese, shredded
- 1/4 tsp paprika
- Salt and pepper to taste
- Olive oil spray for greasing

Directions:

1. Preheat oven to 375°F (190°C)
2. Grease muffin tin cups with olive oil spray
3. In a bowl, whisk eggs with paprika, salt, and pepper
4. Add turkey, spinach, and cheddar cheese
5. Divide into muffin tins and bake for 20 min or until set

Tips:

- Consider using smoked turkey for a flavor boost
- Top with a salsa for a fresh, zesty finish
- Guide to adjust seasoning according to personal sodium intake goals

Nutritional Values: Calories: 130, Fat: 7g, Carbs: 1g, Protein: 15g, Sugar: 0g, Sodium: 220 mg, Potassium: 200 mg, Cholesterol: 195 mg

CHIA AND PUMPKIN SEED POWER BARS

Preparation Time: 15 min
Cooking Time: none

Mode of Cooking: No Cooking
Servings: 10
Ingredients:

- 1 C. oats
- 1/4 C. chia seeds
- 1/2 C. pumpkin seeds
- 1/4 C. flaxseed meal
- 1/3 C. honey
- 1/2 C. peanut butter
- 1 tsp vanilla extract
- 1/4 tsp cinnamon
- 1/8 tsp salt

Directions:

1. Combine oats, chia seeds, pumpkin seeds, flaxseed meal, cinnamon, and salt in a bowl
2. In a separate bowl, mix honey, peanut butter, and vanilla extract until smooth
3. Combine both mixtures and stir until everything is evenly coated
4. Press mixture firmly into a lined baking tray
5. Refrigerate for at least 2 hr until set
6. Cut into bars

Tips:

- Store bars in an airtight container in the refrigerator for up to a week for best freshness
- Optional: add dark chocolate chips or dried fruit for variety

Nutritional Values: Calories: 200, Fat: 12g, Carbs: 18g, Protein: 6g, Sugar: 8g, Sodium: 55 mg, Potassium: 150 mg, Cholesterol: 0 mg

ALMOND COCONUT ENERGY BARS

Preparation Time: 20 min
Cooking Time: none
Mode of Cooking: No Cooking
Servings: 8
Ingredients:

- 1/2 C. raw almonds
- 1/2 C. sunflower seeds
- 1/3 C. shredded unsweetened coconut
- 1/4 C. sesame seeds
- 1/4 C. almond butter
- 1/3 C. coconut oil, melted
- 2 Tbsp maple syrup
- 1/2 tsp vanilla extract

Directions:

1. Blend almonds and sunflower seeds in a food processor until coarsely chopped
2. Add shredded coconut, sesame seeds, almond butter, melted coconut oil, maple syrup, and vanilla extract; pulse until the mixture sticks together
3. Press firmly into a lined square baking dish
4. Chill in the refrigerator for at least 3 hr to set
5. Cut into bars

Tips:

- Bars can be stored in the freezer for up to one month for maintained freshness
- Replace maple syrup with honey for a different sweetness profile

Nutritional Values: Calories: 215, Fat: 18g, Carbs: 10g, Protein: 5g, Sugar: 5g, Sodium: 20 mg, Potassium: 170 mg, Cholesterol: 0 mg

PISTACHIO AND DATE BREAKFAST BARS

Preparation Time: 15 min
Cooking Time: none
Mode of Cooking: No Cooking
Servings: 12
Ingredients:

- 1 C. pitted dates
- 1/2 C. roasted pistachios
- 1/2 C. rolled oats
- 1/3 C. dried cranberries
- 1/4 C. honey
- 1 tsp cinnamon
- 1/4 tsp nutmeg

Directions:

1. Process dates in a food processor until they form a sticky paste
2. Combine date paste with roasted pistachios, rolled oats, dried cranberries, honey, cinnamon, and nutmeg in a mixing bowl
3. Press the mixture evenly into a lined baking pan
4. Refrigerate for about 2-3 hr until set
5. Slice into bars

Tips:

- Use a piece of parchment paper to press the mixture evenly and to avoid sticking
- Swap dried cranberries for raisins or chopped apricots for a different taste

Nutritional Values: Calories: 180, Fat: 8g, Carbs: 26g, Protein: 4g, Sugar: 18g, Sodium: 30 mg, Potassium: 200 mg, Cholesterol: 0 mg

CHAPTER 7: LUNCH RECIPES

As we transition from the energizing beginnings of your day, found in our breakfast recipes, let's delve into the bustling middle—lunchtime. The sun climbs higher, and so does our need for a meal that not only satisfies our midday hunger but also rejuvenates our focus and energy for the hours ahead.

Lunch, often squeezed between meetings or errands, can easily fall prey to convenience over quality. But what if I told you that the DASH diet embraces both? That's right, lunch can be both convenient and conducive to your health goals. In this chapter, we'll explore how to transform your lunches from rushed, forgettable meals into delightful pauses that nourish both body and spirit.

Imagine sitting down to a plate bursting with colors: vibrant greens, radiant oranges, and deep reds. These aren't just pleasing to the eye but packed with nutrients essential for managing blood pressure and boosting your overall health. From fresh and light salads that can be whipped up in minutes to hearty, satisfying sandwiches that taste like leisure, despite their quick assembly – each recipe is designed to fit seamlessly into your busy lifestyle.

But there's more to these lunches than meets the eye. Every recipe in this chapter adheres to the principles of the DASH diet, ensuring they're low in sodium and rich in potassium, magnesium, and calcium. These nutrients are your allies in the fight against high blood pressure, and when combined tastefully, lead to meals that you'll look forward to every day.

Moreover, I understand that lunchtime is not just a solo affair; it's often a meal shared with friends, colleagues, or family. To this end, I've crafted recipes that cater to all palates, ensuring that you're equipped to please a crowd or perhaps introduce someone to the perks of the DASH diet without them even knowing it's "diet food."

So, set aside those concerns about bland or complicated lunch options. The recipes you'll discover here are designed to be straightforward yet flavorful, proving that you can eat well, take care of your heart, and savor every bite, even on the busiest of days. Let's make every lunch count!

1. FRESH AND LIGHT SALADS

MEDITERRANEAN CHICKPEA SALAD WITH SUN-DRIED TOMATOES

Preparation Time: 15 min
Cooking Time: none
Mode of Cooking: No Cooking
Servings: 4
Ingredients:

- 2 cups chickpeas, cooked and drained
- 1 cup cucumber, diced
- ½ cup sun-dried tomatoes, chopped
- ¼ cup red onion, thinly sliced
- ⅓ cup feta cheese, crumbled
- ¼ cup black olives, sliced
- 2 Tbsp extra virgin olive oil
- 1 Tbsp red wine vinegar
- 1 tsp dried oregano
- Salt and pepper to taste

Directions:

1. Combine chickpeas, cucumber, sun-dried tomatoes, red onion, feta cheese, and black olives in a large bowl
2. In a separate small bowl, whisk together olive oil, red wine vinegar, and dried oregano
3. Pour dressing over salad and toss gently to combine
4. Season with salt and pepper to taste

Tips:

- Serve immediately or chill to enhance flavors
- Substitute red wine vinegar with lemon juice for a citrusy twist
- Add fresh parsley or mint for extra freshness

Nutritional Values: Calories: 250, Fat: 11g, Carbs: 33g, Protein: 9g, Sugar: 6g, Sodium: 220 mg, Potassium: 474 mg, Cholesterol: 15 mg

AVOCADO AND CHICKPEA SALAD WITH POMEGRANATE

Preparation Time: 20 min
Cooking Time: none
Mode of Cooking: No Cooking
Servings: 4
Ingredients:

- 1 ripe avocado, pitted and diced
- 1½ cups chickpeas, rinsed and drained
- 1 cup arugula leaves
- ½ cup pomegranate arils
- ¼ cup red bell pepper, finely chopped
- 3 Tbsp olive oil
- 1 Tbsp balsamic vinegar
- 2 tsp honey
- 1 tsp mustard
- Salt and pepper to taste

Directions:

1. In a large bowl, combine avocado, chickpeas, arugula, pomegranate arils, and red bell pepper
2. In a small bowl, whisk together olive oil, balsamic vinegar, honey, and mustard
3. Drizzle the dressing over the salad and toss to coat thoroughly
4. Season with salt and pepper to taste

Tips:

- Can be served as a standalone dish or paired with grilled chicken for extra protein
- Add a sprinkle of goat cheese or feta for a creamy texture

Nutritional Values: Calories: 290, Fat: 19g, Carbs: 27g, Protein: 7g, Sugar: 11g, Sodium: 210 mg, Potassium: 532 mg, Cholesterol: 0 mg

GREEK CHICKPEA SALAD WITH HERBED YOGURT DRESSING

Preparation Time: 10 min
Cooking Time: none
Mode of Cooking: No Cooking
Servings: 4
Ingredients:

- 2 cups chickpeas, drained and rinsed
- 1 cup cherry tomatoes, halved
- ¾ cup cucumber, diced
- ½ cup red onion, finely chopped
- ⅓ cup Kalamata olives, pitted and halved
- ½ cup plain Greek yogurt
- 1 Tbsp lemon juice
- 2 Tbsp fresh dill, chopped
- 1 clove garlic, minced
- Salt and pepper to taste

Directions:

1. In a large mixing bowl, combine chickpeas, cherry tomatoes, cucumber, red onion, and Kalamata olives
2. For the dressing, in a small bowl, mix Greek yogurt, lemon juice, fresh dill, and minced garlic until well blended
3. Pour the dressing over the salad ingredients and toss to coat evenly

4. Season with salt and pepper as needed

Tips:
- Opt for low-fat Greek yogurt to reduce calories
- Serve with whole-wheat pita bread for a satisfying meal

Nutritional Values: Calories: 215, Fat: 6g, Carbs: 32g, Protein: 10g, Sugar: 7g, Sodium: 235 mg, Potassium: 435 mg, Cholesterol: 3 mg

CITRUS KISSED QUINOA AND BLACK BEAN SALAD

Preparation Time: 15 min
Cooking Time: 20 min
Mode of Cooking: Stovetop
Servings: 4
Ingredients:

- 1 C. quinoa, rinsed
- 2 C. water
- 1 can black beans, drained and rinsed
- 1 large orange, segmented and chopped
- 1 small red onion, finely chopped
- 1 bell pepper, diced
- ¼ C. fresh cilantro, chopped
- 2 Tbsp olive oil
- 1 Tbsp lime juice
- 1 tsp cumin
- Salt to taste
- Fresh ground black pepper to taste

Directions:

1. Cook quinoa in water as per instructions until fluffy and water is absorbed
2. In a large bowl, combine the cooked quinoa with black beans, orange segments, red onion, bell pepper, and cilantro
3. In a small bowl, whisk together olive oil, lime juice, cumin, salt, and black pepper
4. Pour dressing over salad and mix well
5. Chill in the refrigerator before serving

Tips:
- Serve with a wedge of lime for an extra zing
- Add diced avocado for richness and creaminess
- For a spicy kick, include a diced jalapeño

Nutritional Values: Calories: 248, Fat: 7g, Carbs: 38g, Protein: 9g, Sugar: 3g, Sodium: 15 mg, Potassium: 431 mg, Cholesterol: 0 mg

MEDITERRANEAN QUINOA AND BLACK BEAN SALAD

Preparation Time: 20 min
Cooking Time: 15 min
Mode of Cooking: Stovetop
Servings: 6
Ingredients:

- 2 C. quinoa, cooked
- 1 can black beans, drained and rinsed
- 1 cucumber, diced
- 1 pt. cherry tomatoes, halved
- ½ C. Kalamata olives, pitted and sliced
- ½ C. feta cheese, crumbled
- ¼ C. fresh parsley, chopped
- 3 Tbsp extra virgin olive oil
- 2 Tbsp red wine vinegar
- 1 garlic clove, minced
- 1 tsp dried oregano
- Salt and pepper to taste

Directions:

1. Combine quinoa, black beans, cucumber, cherry tomatoes, olives, and feta in a large salad bowl
2. In a small bowl, whisk together olive oil, red wine vinegar, minced garlic, oregano, salt, and pepper
3. Pour dressing over salad and toss to combine
4. Allow to sit for 10 minutes before serving to blend flavors

Tips:
- Add a squeeze of lemon for a fresh taste

- Garnish with additional parsley for enhanced flavor and presentation

Nutritional Values: Calories: 265, Fat: 10g, Carbs: 34g, Protein: 12g, Sugar: 2g, Sodium: 210 mg, Potassium: 360 mg, Cholesterol: 17 mg

TROPICAL QUINOA AND BLACK BEAN SALAD

Preparation Time: 10 min
Cooking Time: none
Mode of Cooking: No Cooking
Servings: 4
Ingredients:

- 2 C. cooked quinoa
- 1 can black beans, rinsed and drained
- 1 mango, peeled and diced
- 1 avocado, peeled and diced
- ½ C. shredded coconut, unsweetened
- ¼ C. red bell pepper, diced
- ¼ C. fresh mint, chopped
- 3 Tbsp coconut oil
- 2 Tbsp lime juice
- Salt and pepper to taste

Directions:

1. In a large bowl, combine quinoa, black beans, mango, avocado, coconut, red bell pepper, and mint
2. In a small bowl, whisk together coconut oil and lime juice
3. Season with salt and pepper to taste
4. Drizzle dressing over the salad and toss gently to coat

Tips:

- Chill before serving to meld the flavors
- Top with toasted coconut flakes for added crunch and flavor

Nutritional Values: Calories: 300, Fat: 15g, Carbs: 35g, Protein: 8g, Sugar: 5g, Sodium: 30 mg, Potassium: 490 mg, Cholesterol: 0 mg

TROPICAL SPINACH AND STRAWBERRY SALAD

Preparation Time: 15 min
Cooking Time: none
Mode of Cooking: No Cooking
Servings: 2
Ingredients:

- 2 C. fresh spinach
- 1 C. strawberries, sliced
- 1/2 avocado, cubed
- 1/4 C. macadamia nuts, roasted and chopped
- 1/4 C. feta cheese, crumbled
- 2 Tbsp red onion, thinly sliced
- 1 Tbsp balsamic vinegar
- 2 Tbsp extra virgin olive oil
- 1 tsp honey
- 1/4 tsp freshly ground black pepper
- 1/8 tsp Himalayan pink salt

Directions:

1. Wash and pat dry spinach leaves
2. Slice strawberries and cube avocado
3. In a large bowl, combine spinach, strawberries, avocado, and red onion
4. In a small bowl, whisk together balsamic vinegar, olive oil, honey, black pepper, and salt to make the dressing
5. Drizzle dressing over salad and toss to coat
6. Sprinkle roasted macadamia nuts and crumbled feta cheese on top

Tips:

- Serve immediately for best texture and flavor
- Can substitute macadamia nuts with almonds for a different crunch
- Feta can be replaced with goat cheese for a creamier texture

Nutritional Values: Calories: 265, Fat: 21g, Carbs: 18g, Protein: 5g, Sugar: 12g, Sodium: 180 mg, Potassium: 350 mg, Cholesterol: 15 mg

CITRUS INFUSED SPINACH AND STRAWBERRY SALAD

Preparation Time: 10 min
Cooking Time: none
Mode of Cooking: No Cooking
Servings: 4
Ingredients:

- 3 C. baby spinach
- 1 C. strawberries, quartered
- 1 orange, peeled and segments
- 1/2 C. sliced almonds, toasted
- 1/4 C. dried cranberries
- 2 Tbsp fresh mint, chopped
- for dressing: 3 Tbsp orange juice
- 1 Tbsp lemon juice
- 2 Tbsp extra virgin olive oil
- 1 tsp Dijon mustard
- 1/2 tsp agave syrup
- pinch of salt and black pepper

Directions:

1. Combine spinach, strawberries, orange segments, sliced almonds, dried cranberries, and chopped mint in a large salad bowl
2. In a separate bowl, mix orange juice, lemon juice, olive oil, Dijon mustard, agave syrup, salt, and pepper to form the dressing
3. Pour the dressing over the salad and toss gently to combine

Tips:

- Toss the salad just before serving to keep ingredients fresh and crisp
- Mint can be replaced with basil for a different herbal note
- Add grilled chicken or shrimp for additional protein

Nutritional Values: Calories: 190, Fat: 11g, Carbs: 21g, Protein: 4g, Sugar: 13g, Sodium: 65 mg, Potassium: 320 mg, Cholesterol: 0 mg

SPICY SPINACH AND STRAWBERRY SALAD WITH POPPY SEED DRESSING

Preparation Time: 20 min
Cooking Time: none
Mode of Cooking: No Cooking
Servings: 4
Ingredients:

- 4 C. spinach leaves
- 1 C. strawberries, sliced
- 1/2 red bell pepper, julienned
- 1/4 C. walnut halves, toasted
- 1/4 red onion, thinly sliced
- for dressing: 3 Tbsp apple cider vinegar
- 1 Tbsp honey
- 1 Tbsp poppy seeds
- 1/2 tsp paprika
- 1/4 C. grapeseed oil
- Salt and pepper to taste

Directions:

1. Prepare the vegetables by washing and slicing
2. Toast walnut halves until fragrant
3. For the dressing, whisk together apple cider vinegar, honey, poppy seeds, paprika, grapeseed oil, salt, and pepper in a bowl
4. Combine the spinach, strawberries, bell pepper, onion, and walnuts in a salad bowl
5. Drizzle the salad with the dressing and toss well

Tips:

- Add a pinch of cayenne to the dressing for an extra kick
- Swap walnuts for pecans if preferred for a southern twist
- Dressing can be made ahead and stored in the refrigerator for up to a week

Nutritional Values: Calories: 230, Fat: 20g, Carbs: 12g, Protein: 3g, Sugar: 8g, Sodium: 55 mg, Potassium: 280 mg, Cholesterol: 0 mg

2. Hearty and Satisfying Sandwiches

Classic Grilled Chicken Wraps

Preparation Time: 15 min
Cooking Time: 10 min
Mode of Cooking: Grilling
Servings: 4
Ingredients:

- 2 large chicken breasts, pounded to even thickness
- 1 Tbsp olive oil
- 1 tsp garlic powder
- 1 tsp smoked paprika
- 4 whole wheat tortillas
- 1/2 cup Greek yogurt
- 1 Tbsp honey mustard
- 1 cup fresh spinach leaves
- 1/2 red onion, thinly sliced
- 1 avocado, sliced
- 1/4 cup feta cheese, crumbled

Directions:

1. Season chicken breasts with olive oil, garlic powder, and smoked paprika
2. Preheat grill to medium high heat (375°F/190°C)
3. Grill chicken for 5 min on each side or until cooked through
4. Let chicken rest for a few mins, then slice thinly
5. Spread Greek yogurt mixed with honey mustard on tortillas
6. Layer spinach, red onion, avocado slices, feta, and grilled chicken on tortillas
7. Roll up tightly, securing with toothpicks if necessary
8. Lightly grill the wraps for about 2 min on each side until the tortillas are slightly crispy

Tips:

- Use whole wheat or multi-grain tortillas for added fiber
- Greek yogurt provides a creamy texture while keeping the wraps low in fat

Nutritional Values: Calories: 350, Fat: 15g, Carbs: 28g, Protein: 27g, Sugar: 5g, Sodium: 260mg, Potassium: 500mg, Cholesterol: 75mg

Mediterranean Grilled Chicken Wraps

Preparation Time: 20 min
Cooking Time: 10 min
Mode of Cooking: Grilling
Servings: 4
Ingredients:

- 2 large chicken breasts, seasoned and grilled
- 2 tsp zaatar
- 4 spinach tortillas
- 1/2 cup hummus
- 1/4 cup tzatziki sauce
- 1 small cucumber, thinly sliced
- 1/4 cup kalamata olives, sliced
- 1/4 cup roasted red peppers, sliced
- 1/4 cup crumbled goat cheese

Directions:

1. Season chicken breasts with zaatar and grill until thoroughly cooked
2. Warm tortillas on the grill for about 1 min on each side
3. Spread hummus on each tortilla, then a layer of tzatziki sauce
4. Add grilled chicken, cucumber, kalamata olives, roasted red peppers, and crumbled goat cheese
5. Roll up the tortillas and grill each side for 2 min until marks are visible

Tips:

- Serve with a side of extra tzatziki for dipping
- Kalamata olives and roasted red peppers add a burst of Mediterranean flavors

Nutritional Values: Calories: 360, Fat: 16g, Carbs: 34g, Protein: 24g, Sugar: 5g, Sodium: 290mg, Potassium: 560mg, Cholesterol: 60mg

SPICY THAI CHICKEN WRAPS

Preparation Time: 20 min
Cooking Time: 10 min
Mode of Cooking: Grilling
Servings: 4
Ingredients:

- 2 large chicken breasts, grilled and sliced
- 1 Tbsp sesame oil
- 1 Tbsp sriracha sauce
- 1 Tbsp soy sauce, low sodium
- 4 large rice paper wraps
- 1 cup mixed salad greens
- 1/2 cup shredded carrots
- 1/2 cup sliced bell peppers
- 1/4 cup fresh cilantro leaves
- 1/4 cup crushed peanuts

Directions:

1. Marinate chicken with sesame oil, sriracha, and soy sauce before grilling
2. Grill the chicken and then slice thinly
3. Soak rice paper wraps in warm water until flexible
4. Lay out wraps and distribute mixed greens, carrots, bell peppers, cilantro, and chicken evenly among them
5. Sprinkle crushed peanuts on top
6. Roll tightly and serve fresh

Tips:

- To prevent wraps from tearing, do not overstuff
- The sriracha and soy sauce marinade brings a delightful heat and umami flavor

Nutritional Values: Calories: 290, Fat: 12g, Carbs: 22g, Protein: 25g, Sugar: 3g, Sodium: 330mg, Potassium: 400mg, Cholesterol: 70mg

CLASSIC TURKEY AND AVOCADO SANDWICH

Preparation Time: 15 min
Cooking Time: none
Mode of Cooking: No Cooking
Servings: 2
Ingredients:

- 2 slices whole grain bread
- 4 oz. turkey breast, low-sodium, thinly sliced
- 1 ripe avocado, peeled and sliced
- 1 Tbsp Dijon mustard
- 1/2 cup fresh spinach leaves
- 2 slices tomato
- 1 Tbsp olive oil mayonnaise
- 1 tsp lemon juice
- Salt substitute and pepper to taste

Directions:

1. Spread Dijon mustard and olive oil mayonnaise on each slice of bread
2. Layer spinach leaves, turkey slices, and tomato slices on one slice of bread
3. In a small bowl, mash the avocado with lemon juice, salt substitute, and pepper then spread it on the top of the turkey
4. Close the sandwich with the other slice of bread, press down lightly, and cut in half diagonally

Tips:

- Use whole grain bread for additional fiber
- Adding a pinch of paprika to the avocado mash can enhance the flavor
- Opt for homemade low-sodium turkey breast if possible

Nutritional Values: Calories: 370, Fat: 20g, Carbs: 28g, Protein: 22g, Sugar: 3g, Sodium: 320 mg, Potassium: 650 mg, Cholesterol: 45 mg

MEDITERRANEAN TURKEY WRAP

Preparation Time: 10 min
Cooking Time: none
Mode of Cooking: No Cooking
Servings: 2
Ingredients:

- 2 whole wheat tortillas
- 4 oz. turkey breast, low-sodium, thinly sliced

- ¼ cup hummus
- 4 slices cucumber
- 4 slices bell pepper
- ¼ cup feta cheese, low-fat
- 1 Tbsp red onion, thinly sliced
- 1 Tbsp olives, sliced
- 1 tsp oregano
- 1 tsp olive oil

Directions:

1. Spread hummus evenly on each tortilla
2. Distribute turkey slices across the tortillas
3. Top with cucumber, bell pepper, feta cheese, red onion, and olives
4. Drizzle with olive oil and sprinkle oregano on top
5. Roll up the tortillas tightly and slice in half

Tips:

- Consider grilling the vegetables slightly for a smoky flavor
- Serve with a side of greek yogurt for a creamy addition

Nutritional Values: Calories: 330, Fat: 15g, Carbs: 27g, Protein: 20g, Sugar: 2g, Sodium: 350 mg, Potassium: 300 mg, Cholesterol: 30 mg

AVOCADO TURKEY CLUB SANDWICH

Preparation Time: 20 min
Cooking Time: none
Mode of Cooking: No Cooking
Servings: 1
Ingredients:

- 1 ciabatta roll, whole grain
- 3 oz. turkey breast, low-sodium, sliced
- 2 Tbsp avocado, mashed
- 2 slices turkey bacon, low-sodium, cooked
- 1 leaf romaine lettuce
- 2 slices tomato
- 1 Tbsp mayonnaise, reduced-fat
- Salt substitute and black pepper to taste

Directions:

1. Toast the ciabatta roll lightly
2. Spread mashed avocado and mayonnaise on each half of the ciabatta
3. Layer lettuce, turkey slices, turkey bacon, and tomato slices on the bottom half
4. Season with salt substitute and black pepper
5. Complete the sandwich with the top half of the ciabatta

Tips:

- Try adding a slice of low-fat cheese for extra flavor
- Opt for air-fried turkey bacon to reduce fat content

Nutritional Values: Calories: 450, Fat: 22g, Carbs: 42g, Protein: 25g, Sugar: 5g, Sodium: 540 mg, Potassium: 850 mg, Cholesterol: 60 mg

MEDITERRANEAN VEGGIE HUMMUS PITA

Preparation Time: 15 min.
Cooking Time: none
Mode of Cooking: No Cooking
Servings: 2
Ingredients:

- 2 whole wheat pita breads
- ½ cup hummus
- ¼ cup diced cucumber
- ¼ cup chopped tomatoes
- ¼ cup sliced red onion
- ¼ cup chopped kalamata olives
- 1 Tbsp chopped fresh parsley
- 2 Tbsp crumbled feta cheese
- Drizzle of extra virgin olive oil

Directions:

1. Spread hummus evenly inside each pita bread
2. Stuff with cucumber, tomatoes, red onion, and kalamata olives
3. Top with parsley and feta cheese
4. Drizzle a little olive oil over the fillings

Tips:

- Opt for low-fat feta to reduce overall fat content
- Prepare veggies in advance for a quicker assembly time

Nutritional Values: Calories: 310, Fat: 12g, Carbs: 42g, Protein: 12g, Sugar: 3g, Sodium: 420 mg, Potassium: 180 mg, Cholesterol: 8 mg

SPICY AVOCADO HUMMUS PITA

Preparation Time: 10 min.
Cooking Time: none
Mode of Cooking: No Cooking
Servings: 2
Ingredients:

- 2 whole wheat pita breads
- ½ cup spicy avocado hummus
- ¼ cup shredded carrots
- ¼ cup thinly sliced cabbage
- 2 Tbsp chopped cilantro
- ¼ cup sliced radishes
- 1 Tbsp lime juice

Directions:

1. Spread spicy avocado humus inside each pita bread
2. Add shredded carrots, cabbage, and sliced radishes
3. Sprinkle chopped cilantro and drizzle lime juice over the vegetables

Tips:

- Using spicy hummus adds flavor without the need for added salt
- Lime juice adds a fresh zest and enhances the flavors without extra calories

Nutritional Values: Calories: 290, Fat: 10g, Carbs: 44g, Protein: 9g, Sugar: 4g, Sodium: 380 mg, Potassium: 270 mg, Cholesterol: 0 mg

ROASTED BELL PEPPER AND HUMMUS PITA

Preparation Time: 20 min.
Cooking Time: 5 min.
Mode of Cooking: Roasting
Servings: 2
Ingredients:

- 2 whole wheat pita breads
- ½ cup classic hummus
- ½ cup roasted bell peppers, sliced
- ¼ cup arugula
- 1 Tbsp balsamic reduction
- 2 Tbsp crumbled goat cheese

Directions:

1. Roast sliced bell peppers in the oven at 425°F (218°C) for 5 min
2. Spread hummus inside each pita
3. Lay roasted peppers and arugula inside
4. Drizzle balsamic reduction and sprinkle goat cheese atop

Tips:

- Roasting peppers beforehand can enhance their sweetness and texture
- Balsamic reduction adds depth of flavor with minimal sodium

Nutritional Values: Calories: 320, Fat: 14g, Carbs: 40g, Protein: 12g, Sugar: 5g, Sodium: 360 mg, Potassium: 200 mg, Cholesterol: 6 mg

3. WARM AND COMFORTING SOUPS

SMOKY LENTIL AND SPINACH SOUP

Preparation Time: 15 min
Cooking Time: 45 min
Mode of Cooking: Stovetop
Servings: 4
Ingredients:

- 1 cup dry green lentils
- 1 medium onion, diced
- 2 carrots, chopped

- 2 stalks celery, chopped
- 3 cloves garlic, minced
- 1 tsp smoked paprika
- 1 Tbsp olive oil
- 4 cups vegetable broth, low sodium
- 3 cups water
- 2 cups baby spinach leaves
- 1 tsp dried thyme
- Salt to taste
- Black pepper to taste

Directions:

1. Heat olive oil in a large soup pot over medium heat
2. Add onion, carrot, and celery and sauté until softened, about 5 minutes
3. Stir in garlic and smoked paprika and cook for another minute until fragrant
4. Add lentils, vegetable broth, water, thyme, salt, and pepper
5. Bring to a boil, then reduce heat to low and simmer uncovered for 30 minutes
6. Add spinach and cook for another 15 minutes until the lentils are tender

Tips:

- Stir in a splash of lemon juice before serving to enhance flavors
- Serve with a side of whole-grain bread for a hearty meal

Nutritional Values: Calories: 250, Fat: 4g, Carbs: 38g, Protein: 15g, Sugar: 5g, Sodium: 300 mg, Potassium: 800 mg, Cholesterol: 0 mg

MOROCCAN LENTIL AND VEGGIE STEW

Preparation Time: 20 min
Cooking Time: 1 hr
Mode of Cooking: Stovetop
Servings: 6
Ingredients:

- 2 cups red lentils
- 1 large sweet potato, cubed
- 1 red bell pepper, diced
- 1 zucchini, diced
- 1 onion, chopped
- 3 cloves garlic, minced
- 1 tsp ground cumin
- 1 tsp ground coriander
- 1/2 tsp ground cinnamon
- 1/4 tsp cayenne pepper
- 4 cups low-sodium vegetable broth
- 2 cups diced tomatoes
- 1 tsp honey
- 2 Tbsp olive oil
- Salt and pepper to taste
- Fresh cilantro for garnish

Directions:

1. Heat olive oil in a large pot over medium heat
2. Add onion and garlic, sauté until onion is translucent
3. Add sweet potato, bell pepper, zucchini, and spices, cook for about 10 minutes
4. Pour in vegetable broth and diced tomatoes, bring to a boil
5. Add lentils, reduce heat to low, cover, and simmer for about 45 minutes until lentils and vegetables are tender
6. Stir in honey, adjust salt and pepper to taste
7. Garnish with fresh cilantro before serving

Tips:

- Add a swirl of yogurt on top for extra creaminess
- Pair with a crispy flatbread for a complete meal

Nutritional Values: Calories: 265, Fat: 5g, Carbs: 45g, Protein: 12g, Sugar: 9g, Sodium: 250 mg, Potassium: 900 mg, Cholesterol: 0 mg

ITALIAN LENTIL AND TOMATO SOUP

Preparation Time: 10 min
Cooking Time: 30 min
Mode of Cooking: Stovetop

Servings: 4
Ingredients:

- 1 cup brown lentils
- 1 onion, chopped
- 2 cloves garlic, minced
- 1 carrot, diced
- 1 celery stalk, diced
- 1 tsp dried basil
- 1 tsp dried oregano
- 3 cups low-sodium vegetable broth
- 2 cups crushed tomatoes
- 1 Tbsp balsamic vinegar
- 2 Tbsp olive oil
- Salt and black pepper to taste
- Grated Parmesan cheese, optional for garnish

Directions:

1. Heat olive oil in a pot over medium heat
2. Add onion, carrot, celery, and garlic, sauté until onion is transparent
3. Stir in basil and oregano, cook for 1 minute
4. Add lentils, vegetable broth, and crushed tomatoes, bring to a simmer
5. Cook for about 20 minutes, or until lentils are tender
6. Stir in balsamic vinegar before serving, season with salt and pepper
7. Garnish with grated Parmesan if desired

Tips:

- Serve with a slice of rustic whole-grain bread for dipping
- A sprinkle of chili flakes can add a nice heat

Nutritional Values: Calories: 230, Fat: 7g, Carbs: 33g, Protein: 12g, Sugar: 6g, Sodium: 280 mg, Potassium: 740 mg, Cholesterol: 5 mg

CREAMY TOMATO BASIL SOUP WITH GREEK YOGURT

Preparation Time: 15 min
Cooking Time: 25 min
Mode of Cooking: Stovetop
Servings: 4
Ingredients:

- 2 Tbsp extra virgin olive oil
- 1 large onion, finely chopped
- 3 cloves garlic, minced
- 4 cups fresh tomatoes, chopped
- 1 cup low-sodium vegetable broth
- 1 Tbsp fresh basil, chopped
- 1 tsp dried oregano
- 1/2 cup plain Greek yogurt
- Salt and pepper to taste
- Fresh basil leaves for garnish

Directions:

1. Heat olive oil in a large pot over medium heat
2. Add onion and garlic, sauté until onion is translucent
3. Add chopped tomatoes and broth, bring to a boil, then reduce heat and simmer for 20 min
4. Remove from heat, blend until smooth using an immersion blender
5. Return to heat, stir in Greek yogurt, basil, and oregano, season with salt and pepper, and heat through without boiling

Tips:

- Serve hot garnished with fresh basil leaves for an extra burst of flavor
- Using Greek yogurt adds creaminess without the added fat of cream
- Always use fresh herbs for a brighter flavor

Nutritional Values: Calories: 160, Fat: 7g, Carbs: 20g, Protein: 6g, Sugar: 12g, Sodium: 70 mg, Potassium: 500 mg, Cholesterol: 5 mg

SMOKY ROASTED TOMATO SOUP

Preparation Time: 10 min
Cooking Time: 40 min
Mode of Cooking: Oven and Stovetop
Servings: 6

Ingredients:

- 6 large tomatoes, halved
- 2 red bell peppers, quartered
- 2 Tbsp smoked paprika
- 3 Tbsp olive oil
- 1 large red onion, chopped
- 3 cups low-sodium vegetable broth
- Salt and pepper to taste
- Fresh chives, chopped for garnish

Directions:

1. Preheat oven to 425°F (220°C)
2. Toss tomatoes and bell peppers with smoked paprika and 2 Tbsp olive oil, spread on a baking sheet and roast for 30 min
3. Heat remaining oil in a pot over medium heat, add onion, cook until soft
4. Add roasted tomatoes and peppers to the pot, pour in broth, season with salt and pepper, simmer for 10 min
5. Blend until smooth

Tips:

- Roasting the vegetables brings out their natural sweetness and adds a smoky flavor
- Serve with a sprinkle of chopped chives for a fresh contrast

Nutritional Values: Calories: 130, Fat: 7g, Carbs: 16g, Protein: 3g, Sugar: 9g, Sodium: 55 mg, Potassium: 480 mg, Cholesterol: 0 mg

SPICY TOMATO AND RED LENTIL SOUP

Preparation Time: 10 min
Cooking Time: 30 min
Mode of Cooking: Stovetop
Servings: 4
Ingredients:

- 1 Tbsp coconut oil
- 1 onion, diced
- 2 cloves garlic, minced
- 1 tsp ground cumin
- 1 tsp chili powder
- 1 cup red lentils
- 4 cups low-sodium vegetable stock
- 2 cups diced tomatoes
- 1 Tbsp lime juice
- Salt to taste
- Fresh cilantro for garnish

Directions:

1. Heat coconut oil in a large saucepan over medium heat
2. Add onion and garlic, sauté until onion is translucent
3. Stir in cumin and chili powder, cook for 1 min
4. Add lentils, stock, and tomatoes, bring to a boil, then simmer for 20 min or until lentils are soft
5. Stir in lime juice, season with salt
6. Serve hot, garnished with fresh cilantro

Tips:

- This soup's spiciness can be adjusted by increasing or reducing the amount of chili powder
- Lime juice adds a fresh zest that complements the tomatoes and spices

Nutritional Values: Calories: 180, Fat: 4g, Carbs: 28g, Protein: 9g, Sugar: 6g, Sodium: 60 mg, Potassium: 550 mg, Cholesterol: 0 mg

CHICKEN AND WILD RICE SOUP WITH MUSHROOMS

Preparation Time: 20 min.
Cooking Time: 35 min.
Mode of Cooking: Stovetop
Servings: 6
Ingredients:

- 1 Tbsp olive oil
- 1 medium onion, chopped
- 2 cloves garlic, minced
- 3 stalks celery, diced
- 3 carrots, peeled and diced

- 8 oz. cremini mushrooms, sliced
- 1 cup wild rice blend
- 4 cups low-sodium chicken broth
- 2 cups water
- 2 cups cooked, shredded chicken breast
- 1 tsp dried thyme
- ½ tsp black pepper
- ½ cup low-fat milk
- 2 Tbsp all-purpose flour

Directions:

1. Heat olive oil in a large soup pot over medium heat
2. Sauté onion, garlic, celery, and carrots until tender, about 5 min.
3. Add mushrooms and cook until they release their moisture, about 7 min.
4. Stir in wild rice, chicken broth, water, chicken, thyme, and pepper
5. Bring to a boil, then reduce heat and simmer covered until rice is tender, about 25 min.
6. Whisk together milk and flour until smooth, then stir into soup
7. Cook for an additional 5 min. to thicken soup

Tips:

- Stir occasionally during simmering to prevent sticking
- If soup is too thick, add a little more water to reach desired consistency
- Garnish with fresh parsley before serving for added color and flavor

Nutritional Values: Calories: 245, Fat: 5g, Carbs: 27g, Protein: 21g, Sugar: 4g, Sodium: 140 mg, Potassium: 648 mg, Cholesterol: 45 mg

LEMON HERB CHICKEN AND WILD RICE SOUP

Preparation Time: 15 min.
Cooking Time: 40 min.
Mode of Cooking: Stovetop
Servings: 4

Ingredients:

- 1 Tbsp olive oil
- 1 small yellow onion, diced
- 3 cloves garlic, minced
- 4 cups low-sodium vegetable broth
- 1 lemon, zested and juiced
- 1 cup wild rice, rinsed
- 2 cups diced cooked chicken breast
- ½ cup carrots, finely chopped
- ½ cup celery, finely chopped
- 2 tsp dried basil
- 1 tsp dried oregano
- Salt and pepper to taste
- 2 Tbsp fresh parsley, chopped

Directions:

1. Heat olive oil in a large saucepan over medium heat
2. Add onion and garlic, cook until onion is translucent, about 3 min.
3. Pour in broth, bring to a boil
4. Add lemon zest, lemon juice, wild rice, chicken, carrots, celery, basil, oregano, salt, and pepper
5. Reduce to a simmer and cook until rice is tender, about 30 min.
6. Stir in parsley just before serving

Tips:

- Add additional lemon zest for extra lemony flavor
- Serve hot with a slice of rustic bread for an enriching meal
- Adjust the herbs according to taste, adding more if desired

Nutritional Values: Calories: 210, Fat: 4g, Carbs: 28g, Protein: 17g, Sugar: 3g, Sodium: 80 mg, Potassium: 300 mg, Cholesterol: 40 mg

CREAMY WILD RICE AND MUSHROOM CHICKEN SOUP

Preparation Time: 25 min.
Cooking Time: 45 min.
Mode of Cooking: Stovetop
Servings: 5
Ingredients:

- 1 Tbsp unsalted butter
- 1 onion, finely chopped
- 2 garlic cloves, minced
- 3 celery stalks, chopped
- 300g sliced shiitake mushrooms
- 1 cup wild rice
- 5 cups low-sodium chicken stock
- 200g cooked chicken breast, shredded
- 1 tsp dried thyme
- Fresh ground black pepper to taste
- ½ cup light cream
- 1 Tbsp cornstarch mixed with 2 Tbsp water

Directions:

1. Melt butter in a large pot over medium heat
2. Add onions, garlic, and celery, cook until onion is soft, about 8 min.
3. Add mushrooms and sauté until they are softened, about 10 min.
4. Mix in wild rice, chicken stock, chicken, thyme, and pepper; bring to a boil
5. Simmer covered until rice is fully cooked, about 25 min.
6. Stir in light cream and cornstarch mixture, simmer for another 10 min. or until soup thickens.

Tips:

- For a creamier texture, blend part of the soup before adding the chicken
- Light cream can be replaced with coconut milk for a dairy-free version
- Serve with a lemon wedge to enhance the flavors

Nutritional Values: Calories: 230, Fat: 8g, Carbs: 26g, Protein: 18g, Sugar: 3g, Sodium: 115 mg, Potassium: 357 mg, Cholesterol: 55 mg

Chapter 8: Dinner Recipes

After a long day, the thought of preparing a gourmet dinner can feel daunting. But what if you could whip up a delicious, DASH-friendly meal with ingredients you likely have on hand, and all within the time it takes your favorite show to rerun an episode? Welcome to your evening sanctuary—simple, nutritious, and utterly satisfying meals that align seamlessly with your busy lifestyle and your health goals.

Imagine this: You step into the kitchen, and within minutes, a fragrant pot of Citrus-Infused Chicken Stew simmers on the stove. Or perhaps a Quick Basil and Tomato Pasta is more to your taste tonight, tossed together with ingredients that are as fresh as they are heart-healthy. These aren't just recipes; they are your passport to a hassle-free, relaxing end to any hectic day.

Dinner is more than just a meal. It's a moment to reconnect with family, to unwind, and to nourish not just your body but also your soul. That's why each recipe in this chapter is designed to minimize prep time and cleanup so you can maximize relaxation and enjoyment. Whether you're setting the table for one or a full house, these dishes promise to be crowd-pleasers, offering something for everyone—without straying from your health goals.

With dishes that range from the robust flavors of a One-Pot Spinach and Beef Delight to the subtle, comforting notes of a Creamy Barley Risotto, you'll find that maintaining a balanced diet can indeed be straightforward and scrumptious. Each recipe here respects your time and your dietary needs, ensuring that you stay on track with the DASH diet while still enjoying the pleasures of great food.

Let's turn the page and dive into a world where dinner is not just another meal but a delightful, healthy ritual that you look forward to every day. Here's to evenings filled with good food, laughter, and the simple joy of eating well with ease and pleasure.

1. Simple and Delicious Entrées

Herbed Citrus Salmon with Fennel

Preparation Time: 15 min
Cooking Time: 25 min
Mode of Cooking: Baking
Servings: 4
Ingredients:

- 4 salmon fillets, 6 oz each
- 1 large fennel bulb, thinly sliced
- 2 oranges, thinly sliced
- 2 Tbsp olive oil
- 2 tsp dried dill
- 1 tsp dried thyme
- 1 tsp dried rosemary
- ½ tsp black pepper
- ¼ tsp salt

Directions:

1. Preheat oven to 375°F (190°C)
2. Line a baking sheet with parchment paper and arrange salmon fillets and sliced fennel
3. In a small bowl, mix olive oil, dill, thyme, rosemary, black pepper, and salt
4. Brush the herb mixture over the salmon and fennel
5. Layer orange slices on top of the salmon

6. Bake in the preheated oven until salmon is cooked through, about 25 min

Tips:
- Pair with a light arugula salad for a complete meal
- If you prefer less fennel's anise flavor, substitute it with thinly sliced bell peppers

Nutritional Values: Calories: 280, Fat: 15g, Carbs: 8g, Protein: 29g, Sugar: 3g, Sodium: 200 mg, Potassium: 860 mg, Cholesterol: 60 mg

Maple-Glazed Salmon with Sage

Preparation Time: 10 min
Cooking Time: 20 min
Mode of Cooking: Baking
Servings: 4
Ingredients:

- 4 salmon fillets, 6 oz each
- 3 Tbsp pure maple syrup
- 2 Tbsp Dijon mustard
- 1 Tbsp fresh sage, chopped
- 1 Tbsp olive oil
- 1 tsp garlic powder
- ½ tsp black pepper
- ¼ tsp salt

Directions:

1. Preheat oven to 400°F (204°C)
2. In a bowl, blend maple syrup, Dijon mustard, chopped sage, olive oil, garlic powder, black pepper, and salt to create the glaze
3. Place salmon fillets on a greased baking sheet
4. Generously apply the maple-sage glaze on each fillet
5. Bake until salmon is opaque and flakes easily with a fork, about 20 min

Tips:
- Use leftover glaze as a sauce for side dishes such as steamed vegetables or quinoa
- Maple syrup provides a natural sweetness that complements the savory elements

Nutritional Values: Calories: 295, Fat: 13g, Carbs: 10g, Protein: 30g, Sugar: 7g, Sodium: 210 mg, Potassium: 820 mg, Cholesterol: 55 mg

Pistachio Crusted Salmon

Preparation Time: 15 min
Cooking Time: 15 min
Mode of Cooking: Baking
Servings: 4
Ingredients:

- 4 salmon fillets, 6 oz each
- ½ cup shelled pistachios, finely chopped
- 2 Tbsp parsley, finely chopped
- 1 Tbsp lemon zest
- 2 Tbsp Dijon mustard
- 1 Tbsp olive oil
- ½ tsp black pepper
- ¼ tsp salt

Directions:

1. Preheat oven to 375°F (190°C)
2. Mix pistachios, parsley, lemon zest, black pepper, and salt in a bowl
3. Brush each salmon fillet with Dijon mustard, then press the pistachio mixture onto the top of each fillet to form a crust
4. Drizzle olive oil over the crusted fillets
5. Bake until the crust is golden and salmon is cooked through, about 15 min

Tips:
- This dish pairs wonderfully with a citrus-infused quinoa
- The pistachio crust introduces a delightful crunch that contrasts the tender salmon

Nutritional Values: Calories: 330, Fat: 20g, Carbs: 9g, Protein: 31g, Sugar: 2g, Sodium: 230 mg, Potassium: 850 mg, Cholesterol: 60 mg

Mediterranean Grilled Chicken and Veggie Kabobs

Preparation Time: 20 min
Cooking Time: 15 min

Mode of Cooking: Grilling
Servings: 4
Ingredients:

- 2 lb. chicken breast, cubed
- 1 red bell pepper, large, sliced
- 1 zucchini, medium, sliced
- 1 yellow squash, medium, sliced
- 1 red onion, large chunks
- 2 Tbsp olive oil
- 1 tsp dried oregano
- 1 tsp dried basil
- 2 garlic cloves, minced
- Juice of 1 lemon
- Salt alternative to taste
- Black pepper to taste

Directions:

1. Thread chicken and vegetables alternately onto skewers
2. In a bowl, mix olive oil, oregano, basil, garlic, lemon juice, salt alternative, and black pepper
3. Brush the mixture over skewers
4. Preheat grill to medium-high heat or 375°F (190°C)
5. Grill skewers, turning occasionally, until chicken is cooked through, about 15 min

Tips:

- Marinate chicken and vegetables in the herb mixture for at least 30 min before grilling for enhanced flavors
- Use metal skewers for better heat conduction

Nutritional Values: Calories: 290, Fat: 9g, Carbs: 10g, Protein: 40g, Sugar: 4g, Sodium: 85 mg, Potassium: 650 mg, Cholesterol: 98 mg

LEMON HERB GRILLED CHICKEN WITH ASPARAGUS

Preparation Time: 15 min
Cooking Time: 10 min
Mode of Cooking: Grilling
Servings: 4
Ingredients:

- 4 chicken breasts, boneless and skinless
- 1 lb. asparagus, trimmed
- 2 Tbsp olive oil
- 1 Tbsp fresh rosemary, minced
- 1 Tbsp fresh thyme, minced
- 2 lemons, one juiced and one sliced
- Salt alternative to taste
- Black pepper to taste

Directions:

1. Rub chicken breasts with olive oil, lemon juice, rosemary, thyme, salt alternative, and black pepper
2. Let marinate for 15 min
3. Preheat grill to medium or 350°F (177°C)
4. Grill chicken for about 5 min on each side or until internal temperature reaches 165°F (74°C)
5. Grill asparagus and lemon slices alongside chicken during the last 3 min of cooking

Tips:

- Serve grilled chicken with grilled lemon slices on top for added flavor
- Roll asparagus in remaining marinade before grilling for extra taste

Nutritional Values: Calories: 225, Fat: 7g, Carbs: 8g, Protein: 34g, Sugar: 3g, Sodium: 75 mg, Potassium: 540 mg, Cholesterol: 88 mg

SPICY GRILLED CHICKEN WITH BELL PEPPER SALSA

Preparation Time: 25 min
Cooking Time: 20 min
Mode of Cooking: Grilling
Servings: 4
Ingredients:

- 4 chicken thighs, boneless and skinless
- 2 red bell peppers, diced
- 1 green bell pepper, diced
- 1 jalapeno, minced

- 2 tomatoes, diced
- 1 onion, diced
- 1/4 cup cilantro, chopped
- Juice of 2 limes
- 2 Tbsp olive oil
- 1 tsp chili powder
- 1 tsp paprika
- Salt alternative to taste
- Black pepper to taste

Directions:

1. Combine bell peppers, jalapeno, tomatoes, onion, cilantro, and lime juice to create salsa
2. Season chicken thighs with olive oil, chili powder, paprika, salt alternative, and black pepper
3. Preheat grill to 375°F (190°C)
4. Grill chicken until fully cooked and slightly charred, about 20 min
5. Serve chicken topped with fresh bell pepper salsa

Tips:

- Prepare salsa a few hours in advance to meld flavors
- Grill chicken on a lower heat to avoid burning spices

Nutritional Values: Calories: 320, Fat: 15g, Carbs: 12g, Protein: 35g, Sugar: 7g, Sodium: 90 mg, Potassium: 690 mg, Cholesterol: 142 mg

MEDITERRANEAN QUINOA STUFFED BELL PEPPERS

Preparation Time: 20 min.
Cooking Time: 35 min.
Mode of Cooking: Baking
Servings: 4
Ingredients:

- 4 large bell peppers, tops cut, seeds removed
- 1 cup quinoa, cooked
- 1 cup cherry tomatoes, halved
- ¾ cup crumbled feta cheese
- ¼ cup Kalamata olives, pitted and chopped
- 2 Tbsp fresh basil, chopped
- 1 clove garlic, minced
- 2 Tbsp olive oil
- Salt to taste

Directions:

1. Preheat oven to 375°F (190°C)
2. In a bowl, combine cooked quinoa, cherry tomatoes, feta cheese, Kalamata olives, basil, garlic, and olive oil
3. Mix thoroughly
4. Stuff the mixture evenly into the bell peppers
5. Place stuffed peppers in a baking dish
6. Bake in the preheated oven for 35 min.

Tips:

- Check the peppers occasionally to prevent overcooking
- Serve hot with a drizzle of extra virgin olive oil

Nutritional Values: Calories: 200, Fat: 9g, Carbs: 27g, Protein: 8g, Sugar: 5g, Sodium: 210 mg, Potassium: 470 mg, Cholesterol: 15 mg

QUINOA & TURKEY STUFFED BELL PEPPERS

Preparation Time: 20 min.
Cooking Time: 40 min.
Mode of Cooking: Baking
Servings: 4
Ingredients:

- 4 large bell peppers, tops cut, seeds removed
- 1 cup quinoa, rinsed
- 2 cups water
- 1 Tbsp olive oil
- 1 lb. ground turkey
- 1 medium onion, chopped
- 2 cloves garlic, minced
- 1 tsp cumin
- 1 tsp paprika
- 1 cup tomato sauce, no salt added
- ½ cup low-fat feta cheese, crumbled

- Fresh parsley, chopped for garnish

Directions:

1. Preheat oven to 375°F (190°C)
2. In a saucepan, bring water to a boil, add quinoa, reduce heat to low, cover, and simmer for 15 min. until water is absorbed
3. In a skillet, heat olive oil over medium heat, add onion and garlic, sauté until soft
4. Add ground turkey, cumin, and paprika to the skillet, cook until turkey is browned
5. Stir in cooked quinoa and tomato sauce, mix well
6. Fill each bell pepper with the quinoa-turkey mixture, place in a baking dish
7. Cover with foil and bake for 30 min. Remove foil, sprinkle with feta cheese, and bake uncovered for additional 10 min.
8. Garnish with fresh parsley before serving

Tips:

- Serve with a side of steamed green beans for a complete meal
- If preferred, add a pinch of chili flakes for a spicy kick
- Using different colored bell peppers makes the dish visually appealing

Nutritional Values: Calories: 320, Fat: 10g, Carbs: 35g, Protein: 24g, Sugar: 6g, Sodium: 180 mg, Potassium: 760 mg, Cholesterol: 55 mg

CAULIFLOWER RICE AND BEAN STUFFED PEPPERS

Preparation Time: 15 min.
Cooking Time: 25 min.
Mode of Cooking: Baking
Servings: 4
Ingredients:

- 4 large bell peppers, tops cut, seeds removed
- 3 cups cauliflower rice
- 1 Tbsp olive oil
- 1 can black beans, rinsed and drained
- 1 cup corn, frozen and thawed
- 1 tsp chili powder
- 1 tsp smoked paprika
- ½ cup diced tomatoes, no salt added
- ¼ cup green onions, chopped
- ¼ cup low-sodium vegetable broth
- 1 cup low-fat shredded cheddar cheese

Directions:

1. Preheat oven to 400°F (204°C)
2. In a skillet, heat olive oil over medium heat, add cauliflower rice, cook for 5 min. stirring frequently
3. Add black beans, corn, chili powder, smoked paprika, and diced tomatoes to the skillet, cook for another 5 min.
4. Stir in green onions and vegetable broth, cook until most of the liquid has evaporated
5. Spoon the mixture into each bell pepper, top each with shredded cheese
6. Place stuffed peppers in a baking dish, cover with foil, and bake for 20 min. Remove foil, and bake for an additional 5 min. or until cheese is bubbly

Tips:

- Replace cheddar with Monterey Jack cheese for a different flavor profile
- Can be served with a dollop of low-fat sour cream or Greek yogurt on top for extra creaminess
- Adding a sprinkle of cilantro adds a fresh burst of flavor

Nutritional Values: Calories: 290, Fat: 9g, Carbs: 37g, Protein: 18g, Sugar: 7g, Sodium: 210 mg, Potassium: 647 mg, Cholesterol: 30 mg

2. ONE-POT WONDERS

MEDITERRANEAN QUINOA AND ROASTED VEGETABLE PILAF

Preparation Time: 15 min.
Cooking Time: 30 min.

Mode of Cooking: Roasting and Simmering
Servings: 4
Ingredients:

- 1 cup quinoa, rinsed
- 2 cups water
- 1 cup cherry tomatoes, halved
- 1 medium zucchini, diced
- 1 bell pepper, chopped
- 1 red onion, sliced
- 3 Tbsp olive oil
- Salt to taste
- 1 tsp black pepper
- 1/2 tsp dried oregano
- 1/4 cup fresh basil, chopped
- Lemon zest from 1 lemon

Directions:

1. Preheat oven to 400°F (200°C)
2. Toss tomatoes, zucchini, bell pepper, and onion with 2 Tbsp olive oil, salt, pepper, and oregano
3. Spread on a baking tray and roast for 25 minutes
4. While vegetables roast, heat 1 Tbsp olive oil over medium heat in a pot
5. Add quinoa and toast for 2 minutes
6. Add water and bring to a boil, then reduce heat and simmer covered for 15 minutes
7. Combine cooked quinoa with roasted vegetables, add basil and lemon zest, and stir well

Tips:

- Garnish with crumbled feta if desired for extra flavor
- Serve with a squeeze of fresh lemon juice for added zest

Nutritional Values: Calories: 295, Fat: 10g, Carbs: 45g, Protein: 8g, Sugar: 5g, Sodium: 30 mg, Potassium: 451 mg, Cholesterol: 0 mg

CURRIED COCONUT QUINOA WITH LENTILS

Preparation Time: 10 min.
Cooking Time: 20 min.
Mode of Cooking: Boiling and Simmering
Servings: 4
Ingredients:

- 1 cup quinoa, rinsed
- 1 cup green lentils, rinsed
- 1 Tbsp coconut oil
- 1 onion, finely chopped
- 2 cloves garlic, minced
- 1 Tbsp curry powder
- 1 tsp turmeric
- 1 can (14 oz.) coconut milk
- 2 cups vegetable broth
- 1 tsp salt
- 1/2 tsp black pepper
- 1/2 cup cilantro, chopped

Directions:

1. Heat coconut oil in a large saucepan over medium heat
2. Sauté onion and garlic until soft
3. Stir in curry powder and turmeric and cook for 1 min.
4. Add quinoa, lentils, coconut milk, vegetable broth, salt, and pepper
5. Bring to a boil, reduce heat to low, cover, and simmer for 20 min., or until lentils and quinoa are tender
6. Stir in cilantro before serving

Tips:

- Top with a dollop of yogurt and extra cilantro for enhanced flavors
- Adjust curry powder according to spice preference

Nutritional Values: Calories: 380, Fat: 12g, Carbs: 54g, Protein: 14g, Sugar: 3g, Sodium: 350 mg, Potassium: 720 mg, Cholesterol: 0 mg

GARLIC MUSHROOM AND SPINACH QUINOA

Preparation Time: 10 min.
Cooking Time: 25 min.
Mode of Cooking: Sautéing and Simmering
Servings: 4
Ingredients:

- 1 cup quinoa, rinsed
- 2 cups vegetable broth
- 2 Tbsp olive oil
- 1 lb. mushrooms, sliced
- 3 cloves garlic, minced
- 4 cups spinach leaves
- 1/2 tsp salt
- 1/4 tsp black pepper
- Grated Parmesan cheese, for serving

Directions:

1. Heat olive oil in a skillet over medium heat
2. Add mushrooms and garlic, sauté until mushrooms are golden
3. Add quinoa and vegetable broth, bring to a boil, then reduce heat and simmer for 20 min.
4. Stir in spinach, salt, and pepper, cook until spinach is wilted
5. Serve with grated Parmesan cheese on top

Tips:

- Use a variety of mushrooms like cremini or shiitake for deeper flavor
- Garnish with toasted pine nuts for a crunch

Nutritional Values: Calories: 280, Fat: 10g, Carbs: 39g, Protein: 11g, Sugar: 2g, Sodium: 400 mg, Potassium: 697 mg, Cholesterol: 5 mg

SUNDRIED TOMATO AND GARLIC CHICKEN STEW

Preparation Time: 15 min
Cooking Time: 4 hr
Mode of Cooking: Slow Cooker
Servings: 6
Ingredients:

- 2 lb. chicken breasts, boneless and skinless, cubed
- 1 cup sundried tomatoes, not in oil, chopped
- 3 cloves garlic, minced
- 1 large onion, diced
- 1 red bell pepper, diced
- 2 carrots, sliced
- 2 celery stalks, chopped
- 4 cups low-sodium chicken broth
- 1 tsp dried basil
- 1 tsp dried oregano
- ½ tsp freshly ground black pepper
- 1 tsp smoked paprika
- 2 Tbsp cornstarch mixed with 2 Tbsp water

Directions:

1. Place all ingredients except cornstarch mixture into the slow cooker and stir to combine
2. Cook on low for 4 hr
3. In the last 30 minutes of cooking, stir in cornstarch mixture to thicken the stew

Tips:

- Use lean cuts of chicken for a healthier option
- Garnish with fresh parsley before serving for a fresh flavor boost
- Serve over a bed of cooked quinoa for a complete meal

Nutritional Values: Calories: 345, Fat: 6g, Carbs: 35g, Protein: 33g, Sugar: 15g, Sodium: 330 mg, Potassium: 1050 mg, Cholesterol: 75 mg

COCONUT CURRY CHICKEN STEW

Preparation Time: 20 min
Cooking Time: 6 hr
Mode of Cooking: Slow Cooker
Servings: 4
Ingredients:

- 1.5 lb. chicken breasts, boneless and skinless

- 1 large sweet potato, peeled and cubed
- 1 cup frozen peas
- 1 onion, chopped
- 2 garlic cloves, minced
- 1 Tbsp fresh ginger, grated
- 1 can (13.5 oz) light coconut milk
- 2 Tbsp curry powder
- 1 tsp turmeric
- ½ cup low-sodium vegetable broth
- 1 cup spinach leaves
- Salt and pepper to taste

Directions:
1. Add all ingredients except for spinach to the slow cooker and stir well
2. Cook on low for 6 hr
3. Stir in spinach just before serving and allow it to wilt

Tips:
- Freeze leftover stew in individual servings for a quick reheat
- Top with chopped cilantro for an extra burst of freshness
- Adjust the amount of curry powder based on your spice preference

Nutritional Values: Calories: 310, Fat: 12g, Carbs: 25g, Protein: 28g, Sugar: 7g, Sodium: 350 mg, Potassium: 890 mg, Cholesterol: 65 mg

MUSHROOM AND BARLEY CHICKEN STEW

Preparation Time: 10 min
Cooking Time: 5 hr
Mode of Cooking: Slow Cooker
Servings: 5
Ingredients:

- 1 lb. chicken thighs, boneless and skinless
- ¾ cup pearl barley
- 1 lb. mixed mushrooms, sliced
- 1 onion, diced
- 2 garlic cloves, minced
- 4 cups low-sodium beef broth
- 1 Tbsp Worcestershire sauce
- 1 tsp dried thyme
- ½ tsp black pepper
- 2 Tbsp fresh parsley, chopped

Directions:
1. Combine all ingredients except parsley in the slow cooker
2. Cook on low for 5 hr
3. Stir in fresh parsley just before serving

Tips:
- Opt for pearl barley for its heartier texture and nutty flavor
- Pair with a fresh green salad for a balanced meal
- Lightly toast barley before adding to the slow cooker to enhance its flavor

Nutritional Values: Calories: 295, Fat: 8g, Carbs: 35g, Protein: 20g, Sugar: 3g, Sodium: 340 mg, Potassium: 650 mg, Cholesterol: 95 mg

MEDITERRANEAN BLISS BAKED COD

Preparation Time: 15 min
Cooking Time: 25 min
Mode of Cooking: Baking
Servings: 4
Ingredients:

- 4 cod fillets, 6 oz. each
- 2 cups cherry tomatoes, halved
- 1 bell pepper, sliced
- 1 zucchini, sliced
- 1 small red onion, chopped
- 3 cloves garlic, minced
- 2 Tbsp olive oil
- 1 tsp dried oregano
- 1 tsp dried basil
- ½ lemon, juiced
- Salt substitute and freshly ground pepper to taste
- ¼ cup fresh basil, chopped

Directions:

1. Preheat oven to 375°F (190°C)
2. Toss vegetables with olive oil, garlic, dried oregano, dried basil, salt substitute, and pepper in a large baking dish
3. Place cod fillets on top of the vegetables
4. Drizzle lemon juice over cod
5. Bake in preheated oven until fish flakes easily with a fork, about 25 min
6. Garnish with fresh basil before serving

Tips:

- Mix different herbs to enhance flavor without adding sodium
- Utilize parchment paper to cover the dish for a steamed effect, preserving flavors and moisture

Nutritional Values: Calories: 240, Fat: 8g, Carbs: 10g, Protein: 34g, Sugar: 4g, Sodium: 70 mg, Potassium: 780 mg, Cholesterol: 60 mg

SPICED ORANGE COD DELIGHT

Preparation Time: 20 min
Cooking Time: 35 min
Mode of Cooking: Baking
Servings: 4
Ingredients:

- 4 cod fillets, 6 oz. each
- 2 oranges, sliced thin
- 1 fennel bulb, thinly sliced
- 2 Tbsp olive oil
- 1 tsp cumin
- 1 tsp paprika
- ¼ tsp cayenne pepper
- Salt substitute and freshly ground black pepper to taste
- Fresh dill for garnish

Directions:

1. Preheat oven to 400°F (204°C)
2. Arrange half of the orange slices and all fennel slices in a baking dish and drizzle with half olive oil
3. Season cod with cumin, paprika, cayenne, salt substitute, and black pepper
4. Place seasoned cod over orange and fennel bed
5. Top cod with remaining orange slices
6. Drizzle remaining olive oil
7. Bake until cod is cooked through, about 35 min
8. Garnish with fresh dill

Tips:

- Use different citrus like lemon or grapefruit for variations in flavor
- Cover the dish with aluminum foil for the first 20 min to keep moisture in
- Spice levels can be adjusted according to taste

Nutritional Values: Calories: 265, Fat: 9g, Carbs: 15g, Protein: 34g, Sugar: 7g, Sodium: 55 mg, Potassium: 840 mg, Cholesterol: 60 mg

HERB-INFUSED COD AND ASPARAGUS

Preparation Time: 10 min
Cooking Time: 20 min
Mode of Cooking: Baking
Servings: 4
Ingredients:

- 4 cod fillets, 6 oz. each
- 1 lb asparagus, trimmed
- 1 lemon, sliced
- 2 Tbsp olive oil
- 1 tsp rosemary, minced
- 1 tsp thyme, minced
- Salt substitute to taste
- Fresh parsley, chopped for garnish

Directions:

1. Preheat oven to 350°F (177°C)
2. Arrange asparagus in a single layer in a baking dish

3. Place cod fillets on top
4. Top with lemon slices and drizzle with olive oil
5. Sprinkle minced rosemary and thyme
6. Season with salt substitute
7. Bake in preheated oven until asparagus is tender and cod flakes easily, about 20 min
8. Garnish with chopped parsley before serving

Tips:

- Experiment with different herbs such as dill or marjoram for a new taste
- Lemon can be replaced with lime for a tangy twist
- Asparagus can be substituted with green beans or snap peas

Nutritional Values: Calories: 190, Fat: 7g, Carbs: 8g, Protein: 28g, Sugar: 3g, Sodium: 55 mg, Potassium: 650 mg, Cholesterol: 60 mg

3. PASTA AND GRAIN DISHES

WHOLE WHEAT PASTA PRIMAVERA WITH SPRING VEGETABLES

Preparation Time: 15 min.
Cooking Time: 20 min.
Mode of Cooking: Stove top
Servings: 4
Ingredients:

- 8 oz. whole wheat spaghetti
- 1 Tbsp olive oil
- 2 cloves garlic, minced
- 1 cup fresh asparagus, trimmed and cut into 2-inch pieces
- 1 medium zucchini, thinly sliced
- 1 cup cherry tomatoes, halved
- 1 yellow bell pepper, sliced
- 1/4 cup peas
- 1/4 cup grated Parmesan cheese
- 1 tsp dried basil
- Salt and pepper to taste

Directions:

1. Cook pasta according to package directions until al dente; drain and set aside
2. Heat olive oil in a large skillet over medium heat
3. Add garlic; sauté for 1 min.
4. Add asparagus, zucchini, tomatoes, bell pepper, and peas; cook, stirring occasionally, until vegetables are tender, about 8-10 min.
5. Toss cooked pasta with the vegetables, Parmesan, and basil; season with salt and pepper
6. Serve warm

Tips:

- Opt for fresh, seasonal vegetables for the best flavor and nutrition
- Grate your own Parmesan for fresher taste
- Add a squeeze of fresh lemon juice before serving for extra zest

Nutritional Values: Calories: 320, Fat: 7g, Carbs: 53g, Protein: 12g, Sugar: 5g, Sodium: 190 mg, Potassium: 374 mg, Cholesterol: 4 mg

CREAMY AVOCADO WHOLE WHEAT PASTA

Preparation Time: 10 min.
Cooking Time: 15 min.
Mode of Cooking: Stove top
Servings: 4
Ingredients:

- 8 oz. whole wheat fettuccine
- 1 ripe avocado, pitted and peeled
- 1/2 cup fresh basil leaves
- 2 Tbsp pine nuts
- 2 cloves garlic, minced
- 2 Tbsp lemon juice
- 1/3 cup extra virgin olive oil
- Salt and pepper to taste
- Parmesan shavings for garnish

Directions:

1. Cook pasta according to package directions until al dente; drain and set aside
2. In a food processor, combine avocado, basil, pine nuts, garlic, and lemon juice; pulse until smooth
3. With the processor running, slowly add olive oil until emulsified
4. Toss pasta with avocado sauce; season with salt and pepper
5. Garnish with Parmesan shavings
6. Serve immediately

Tips:

- Toast pine nuts for added crunch and nuttiness
- Use high-quality EVOO for a smoother sauce
- Garnish with additional fresh basil if desired

Nutritional Values: Calories: 485, Fat: 30g, Carbs: 49g, Protein: 10g, Sugar: 2g, Sodium: 20 mg, Potassium: 595 mg, Cholesterol: 2 mg

MEDITERRANEAN WHOLE WHEAT PASTA TOSS

Preparation Time: 12 min.
Cooking Time: 18 min.
Mode of Cooking: Stove top
Servings: 4
Ingredients:

- 8 oz. whole wheat penne
- 1 Tbsp olive oil
- 2 cloves garlic, minced
- 1/2 cup canned artichoke hearts, drained and chopped
- 1/2 cup black olives, sliced
- 1/2 cup sun-dried tomatoes, chopped
- 1/4 cup crumbled feta cheese
- 1/4 cup fresh parsley, chopped
- Juice of 1 lemon
- Salt and pepper to taste

Directions:

1. Cook pasta according to package directions until al dente; drain and set aside
2. In a skillet, heat olive oil over medium heat
3. Add garlic; sauté for 1 min.
4. Add artichoke hearts, olives, and sun-dried tomatoes; cook for 5-7 min.
5. Remove from heat; toss with pasta, feta, parsley, and lemon juice; season with salt and pepper
6. Serve warm

Tips:

- Incorporate capers for a briny depth of flavor
- Use oil from the sun-dried tomatoes for extra richness
- Crumble feta just before serving to maintain its texture

Nutritional Values: Calories: 358, Fat: 15g, Carbs: 48g, Protein: 12g, Sugar: 4g, Sodium: 560 mg, Potassium: 450 mg, Cholesterol: 8 mg

CLASSIC BARLEY AND MUSHROOM RISOTTO

Preparation Time: 10 min
Cooking Time: 35 min
Mode of Cooking: Stovetop
Servings: 4
Ingredients:

- 1 cup pearled barley
- 1 Tbsp olive oil
- 2 cloves garlic, minced
- 1 onion, finely chopped
- 8 oz cremini mushrooms, sliced
- 4 cups low-sodium vegetable broth
- ½ cup parmesan cheese, grated
- 1 Tbsp fresh thyme
- Salt and pepper to taste

Directions:

1. Heat olive oil in a large saucepan over medium heat
2. Sauté garlic and onion until translucent

3. Add mushrooms and cook until they begin to release their juices
4. Stir in barley and cook for another 2 min
5. Add 1 cup broth and stir continuously until fully absorbed, repeat with remaining broth
6. Once barley is tender and creamy, remove from heat, stir in parmesan and thyme, season with salt and pepper

Tips:

- To enhance flavor, use freshly grated parmesan
- Stir frequently to prevent sticking and encourage creaminess

Nutritional Values: Calories: 350, Fat: 8g, Carbs: 58g, Protein: 14g, Sugar: 3g, Sodium: 200 mg, Potassium: 410 mg, Cholesterol: 10 mg

BARLEY RISOTTO WITH ASPARAGUS AND LEMON

Preparation Time: 15 min
Cooking Time: 40 min
Mode of Cooking: Stovetop
Servings: 4
Ingredients:

- 1 cup pearled barley
- 1 Tbsp olive oil
- 1 small leek, finely chopped
- 2 cups diced asparagus
- 4 cups low-sodium chicken broth
- Zest and juice of 1 lemon
- ½ cup feta cheese, crumbled
- Salt and pepper to taste

Directions:

1. Heat olive oil in a large skillet over medium heat
2. Add leeks and cook until soft
3. Stir in barley and sauté for 3 min
4. Add broth 1 cup at a time, allowing each addition to be absorbed before adding the next
5. In the last 5 min of cooking, add asparagus
6. Remove from heat and mix in lemon zest, lemon juice, and feta cheese
7. Season with salt and pepper

Tips:

- Add lemon at the end of cooking to preserve its vibrant flavor
- Feta can be substituted with goat cheese for a creamier texture

Nutritional Values: Calories: 320, Fat: 9g, Carbs: 52g, Protein: 12g, Sugar: 5g, Sodium: 240 mg, Potassium: 370 mg, Cholesterol: 15 mg

MUSHROOM AND SPINACH BARLEY RISOTTO

Preparation Time: 10 min
Cooking Time: 30 min
Mode of Cooking: Stovetop
Servings: 4
Ingredients:

- 1 cup pearled barley
- 1 Tbsp olive oil
- 2 shallots, minced
- 200g baby spinach
- 300g button mushrooms, sliced
- 4 cups low-sodium beef broth
- ¼ cup dry white wine
- ¼ cup mascarpone cheese
- Salt and pepper to taste

Directions:

1. Heat oil in a pot over medium flame
2. Cook shallots until tender
3. Add mushrooms and sauté until golden
4. Deglaze the pan with wine and reduce for 3 min
5. Add barley, gradually mix in broth until fully absorbed and barley is creamy
6. Stir in spinach just before serving, add mascarpone, season with salt and pepper

Tips:
- Use dry white wine to intensify umami flavors in mushrooms
- Stirring often promotes a creamier texture without additional fat

Nutritional Values: Calories: 370, Fat: 12g, Carbs: 55g, Protein: 12g, Sugar: 4g, Sodium: 210 mg, Potassium: 495 mg, Cholesterol: 20 mg

GINGER-SESAME BROWN RICE WITH EDAMAME

Preparation Time: 15 min
Cooking Time: 25 min
Mode of Cooking: Stovetop
Servings: 4
Ingredients:

- 2 cups water
- 1 cup brown rice
- 1 cup shelled edamame, fresh or frozen
- 1 red bell pepper, diced
- 2 Tbsp sesame seeds
- 1 Tbsp sesame oil
- 2 Tbsp fresh ginger, minced
- 2 cloves garlic, minced
- 1 Tbsp soy sauce, low sodium
- ¼ cup green onions, sliced

Directions:

1. Bring water to a boil in a medium saucepan, add rice, reduce to simmer, cover, and cook for 20 min
2. In a separate pan, sauté ginger and garlic in sesame oil over medium heat for 2 min
3. Add bell pepper and edamame, cook for an additional 3 min
4. Stir in cooked rice, soy sauce, and sesame seeds
5. Cook together for 2 min
6. Garnish with green onions just before serving

Tips:
- Use tamari instead of soy sauce for a gluten-free option
- Toast the sesame seeds before adding to enhance their flavor
- Add a pinch of chili flakes for a spicy kick

Nutritional Values: Calories: 235, Fat: 10g, Carbs: 31g, Protein: 9g, Sugar: 3g, Sodium: 170 mg, Potassium: 460 mg, Cholesterol: 0 mg

COCONUT-LIME BROWN RICE WITH CASHEWS

Preparation Time: 10 min
Cooking Time: 40 min
Mode of Cooking: Stovetop
Servings: 4
Ingredients:

- 1 cup brown rice
- 2 cups coconut milk
- 1 lime, zest and juice
- ½ cup cashews, roughly chopped
- 1 Tbsp olive oil
- ¼ tsp salt, optional
- 1 Tbsp cilantro, chopped

Directions:

1. Bring coconut milk to a boil, add rice, stir, reduce heat to low, cover, and cook for about 40 min or until rice is tender
2. In a small skillet, toast the cashews in olive oil over medium heat until golden, stirring frequently
3. Once rice is cooked, stir in lime zest, lime juice, and salt
4. Sprinkle with toasted cashews and fresh cilantro before serving

Tips:
- Rinse brown rice before cooking to remove excess starch
- For a richer flavor, add a tablespoon of coconut oil to the rice before cooking

- Serve with grilled chicken or steamed vegetables for a complete meal

Nutritional Values: Calories: 300, Fat: 18g, Carbs: 28g, Protein: 6g, Sugar: 1g, Sodium: 65 mg, Potassium: 260 mg, Cholesterol: 0 mg

SPICY TOMATO BASIL BROWN RICE

Preparation Time: 5 min
Cooking Time: 30 min
Mode of Cooking: Stovetop
Servings: 4
Ingredients:

- 1 cup brown rice
- 2 cups vegetable broth, low sodium
- 1 cup cherry tomatoes, halved
- 1 tsp red chili flakes
- 2 garlic cloves, minced
- 1 Tbsp olive oil
- ½ cup basil leaves, fresh, chopped
- ¼ cup grated Parmesan cheese, optional

Directions:

1. Cook brown rice in vegetable broth according to package instructions
2. In a skillet, heat olive oil over medium heat, add garlic and chili flakes, sauté for 1 min
3. Add tomatoes and cook until softened, about 5 min
4. Mix cooked rice with sautéed tomatoes and basil
5. Top with grated Parmesan before serving

Tips:

- Serve this dish with a side of steamed green beans for a balanced meal
- Basil can be substituted with spinach for a variation
- Adding a dash of balsamic vinegar can enhance the flavor

Nutritional Values: Calories: 215, Fat: 5g, Carbs: 35g, Protein: 7g, Sugar: 2g, Sodium: 55 mg, Potassium: 275 mg, Cholesterol: 5 mg

CHAPTER 9: SNACK AND APPETIZER RECIPES

Snacking — often seen as a pitfall in many diets, can actually be a golden opportunity on your journey with the DASH diet. I think we've all had that moment, somewhere between one meal and the next, when hunger strikes unexpectedly. It's easy to reach for whatever is nearest, but what if I told you that with a little bit of prep, your between-meal bites could be just as nourishing and delightful as your main dishes?

In this chapter, we delve into the world of snacks and appetizers that are not only easy to prepare but are also perfectly aligned with the DASH diet principles. These are recipes that you can whip up in a flash, serve at a family gathering, or simply enjoy on a quiet evening at home. They're designed to keep you satisfied, maintain your energy levels, and of course, help manage your blood pressure — all without compromising on taste or indulgence.

Imagine coming home after a long day, and in just a few minutes, you have a delicious, heart-healthy appetizer ready to enjoy. Or picture yourself hosting a gathering where everyone raves about the tasty, healthy snacks — with no one guessing they're specifically designed to be low in sodium and rich in nutrients.

The beauty of these recipes lies in their simplicity and flexibility. From zesty dips to crunchy, fresh veggie platters, and even a few surprising sweets, there's something here to satisfy every craving. Each recipe packs a punch of flavor using herbs, spices, and DASH-friendly ingredients that turn ordinary snacks into extraordinary treats.

Remember, the key to successful snacking on the DASH diet is not just about what you eat, but how you eat. It's about making mindful choices that fit effortlessly into your lifestyle, supporting your health without the need for complex preparations or obscure ingredients.

So, let's set the table with some delicious, wholesome appetizers and snacks that promise to make your DASH diet journey both pleasurable and sustainable. After all, every bite is an opportunity to nourish and delight!

1. HEALTHY SNACKS

SPICED MAPLE CINNAMON NUT MIX

Preparation Time: 10 min
Cooking Time: 15 min
Mode of Cooking: Baking
Servings: 6

Ingredients:

- 1 C. almonds
- 1 C. walnuts
- 1 C. pecans
- 2 Tbsp pure maple syrup
- 1 tsp ground cinnamon
- ½ tsp ground nutmeg
- ¼ tsp cayenne pepper
- 1 Tbsp olive oil
- ¼ tsp salt

Directions:

1. Preheat oven to 350°F (175°C)
2. In a large bowl, combine nuts with maple syrup, olive oil, cinnamon, nutmeg, cayenne pepper, and salt
3. Spread the mixture evenly on a baking sheet

4. Bake for 15 min, stirring halfway through

Tips:

- Stir nuts again after removing from oven to avoid sticking
- Let cool completely before serving to enhance flavor integration

Nutritional Values: Calories: 210, Fat: 20g, Carbs: 9g, Protein: 5g, Sugar: 4g, Sodium: 100 mg, Potassium: 125 mg, Cholesterol: 0 mg

SESAME SEED & CHIA ENERGY BITES

Preparation Time: 15 min
Cooking Time: none
Mode of Cooking: No Cooking
Servings: 8
Ingredients:

- 1 C. rolled oats
- ½ C. chia seeds
- ½ C. sesame seeds, toasted
- 1/3 C. honey
- ½ C. peanut butter
- 1 tsp vanilla extract
- 1 pinch salt

Directions:

1. In a medium bowl, mix rolled oats, chia seeds, and sesame seeds
2. Add honey, peanut butter, vanilla extract, and salt and combine until the mixture is sticky
3. Form into small balls and chill in the refrigerator until firm

Tips:

- Can be stored in an airtight container for up to a week
- For a nuttier flavor, roast the sesame seeds lightly before mixing

Nutritional Values: Calories: 180, Fat: 10g, Carbs: 20g, Protein: 5g, Sugar: 10g, Sodium: 70 mg, Potassium: 130 mg, Cholesterol: 0 mg

PISTACHIO & CRANBERRY SALT-FREE TRAIL MIX

Preparation Time: 5 min
Cooking Time: none
Mode of Cooking: Mixing
Servings: 4
Ingredients:

- 1 C. pistachios, shelled and unsalted
- ½ C. dried cranberries, unsweetened
- ½ C. coconut flakes, unsweetened
- ¼ C. pumpkin seeds, raw

Directions:

1. Combine pistachios, dried cranberries, coconut flakes, and pumpkin seeds in a large bowl and mix well

Tips:

- This mix can be customized with any other favorite nuts or seeds
- Keep in an airtight container to maintain freshness

Nutritional Values: Calories: 230, Fat: 15g, Carbs: 20g, Protein: 7g, Sugar: 15g, Sodium: 5 mg, Potassium: 290 mg, Cholesterol: 0 mg

APPLE SLICES WITH ALMOND-CINNAMON BUTTER

Preparation Time: 5 min.
Cooking Time: none
Mode of Cooking: No Cooking
Servings: 2
Ingredients:

- 1 large apple, cored and sliced
- 2 Tbsp almond butter
- 1 tsp honey (optional)
- 1/4 tsp ground cinnamon

Directions:

2. Combine almond with ground cinnamon and honey in a small bowl
3. Spread the mixture on each apple slice

Tips:

- Use a corer to easily slice the apples
- Opt for a drizzle of honey for added sweetness but skip if cutting back on sugar

Nutritional Values: Calories: 180, Fat: 8g, Carbs: 27g, Protein: 4g, Sugar: 21g, Sodium: 2 mg, Potassium: 300 mg, Cholesterol: 0 mg

BANANA MEDALLIONS WITH PEANUT BUTTER AND FLAXSEEDS

Preparation Time: 10 min.
Cooking Time: none
Mode of Cooking: No Cooking
Servings: 2
Ingredients:

- 1 ripe banana, sliced
- 2 Tbsp natural peanut butter
- 1 Tbsp ground flaxseeds
- A pinch of sea salt

Directions:

1. Spread peanut butter over each banana slice
2. Sprinkle ground flaxseeds and a pinch of sea salt on top

Tips:

- Choose ripe bananas for natural sweetness
- Store unused banana slices in an airtight container in the refrigerator

Nutritional Values: Calories: 210, Fat: 14g, Carbs: 20g, Protein: 7g, Sugar: 10g, Sodium: 100 mg, Potassium: 450 mg, Cholesterol: 0 mg

PEAR WEDGES WITH CASHEW VANILLA SPREAD

Preparation Time: 8 min.
Cooking Time: none
Mode of Cooking: No Cooking
Servings: 3
Ingredients:

- 2 ripe pears, cored and cut into wedges
- 3 Tbsp cashew butter
- 1/2 tsp vanilla extract
- 1 Tbsp honey (optional)

Directions:

1. Mix cashew butter with vanilla extract and optional honey for sweetness in a small bowl
2. Spread evenly on pear wedges

Tips:

- Serve immediately to avoid browning of pears
- If preferred, sprinkle with a touch of cinnamon for extra flavor

Nutritional Values: Calories: 155, Fat: 8g, Carbs: 22g, Protein: 2g, Sugar: 16g, Sodium: 3 mg, Potassium: 170 mg, Cholesterol: 0 mg

CLASSIC CARROT AND CUCUMBER STICKS WITH SPICED HUMMUS

Preparation Time: 10 min
Cooking Time: none
Mode of Cooking: No Cooking
Servings: 4
Ingredients:

- 2 large cucumbers, washed and cut into sticks
- 4 medium carrots, peeled and cut into sticks
- 1 can (15 oz.) chickpeas, drained and rinsed
- 2 Tbsp tahini
- 3 Tbsp lemon juice
- 1 clove garlic, minced
- ½ tsp cumin
- ¼ tsp smoked paprika
- ¼ tsp salt
- 2 Tbsp olive oil
- 2 Tbsp water

Directions:

1. Combine chickpeas, tahini, lemon juice, garlic, cumin, smoked paprika, salt, olive oil, and water in a blender or food processor and blend until smooth
2. Arrange carrot and cucumber sticks on a serving platter
3. Serve with hummus dip on the side

Tips:

- Add roasted red peppers to the hummus for a sweet note
- Serve hummus chilled for a refreshing snack

Nutritional Values: Calories: 187, Fat: 8g, Carbs: 25g, Protein: 6g, Sugar: 5g, Sodium: 198 mg, Potassium: 362 mg, Cholesterol: 0 mg

ZESTY BELL PEPPER STICKS WITH AVOCADO LIME HUMMUS

Preparation Time: 15 min
Cooking Time: none
Mode of Cooking: No Cooking
Servings: 4
Ingredients:

- 2 red bell peppers, washed and cut into sticks
- 2 yellow bell peppers, washed and cut into sticks
- 1 ripe avocado, pitted and peeled
- 1 can (15 oz.) white beans, drained and rinsed
- 2 Tbsp lime juice
- 1 clove garlic, minced
- ¼ tsp chili flakes
- ¼ tsp salt
- 1 Tbsp olive oil
- 2 Tbsp water

Directions:

1. Mash the avocado in a bowl until smooth
2. Add white beans, lime juice, garlic, chili flakes, and salt to the mashed avocado and mix well
3. Gradually stir in olive oil and water until the mixture achieves a creamy consistency
4. Serve the mixture as a dip with bell pepper sticks arranged around it

Tips:

- Incorporate a pinch of cilantro into the hummus for a fresh twist
- Keep the dip covered in the refrigerator to prevent browning

Nutritional Values: Calories: 204, Fat: 11g, Carbs: 22g, Protein: 7g, Sugar: 3g, Sodium: 202 mg, Potassium: 520 mg, Cholesterol: 0 mg

SNAP PEA CRISPS WITH CURRY YOGURT DIP

Preparation Time: 12 min
Cooking Time: none
Mode of Cooking: No Cooking
Servings: 4
Ingredients:

- 2 cups snap peas, washed and dried
- 1 cup plain Greek yogurt
- 1 Tbsp curry powder
- 1 tsp honey
- ¼ tsp salt
- 1 Tbsp lemon juice
- Fresh mint leaves for garnish

Directions:

1. Combine Greek yogurt, curry powder, honey, salt, and lemon juice in a small bowl and mix until well incorporated
2. Arrange snap peas on a serving tray
3. Serve with curry yogurt dip garnished with mint leaves

Tips:

- Add a sprinkle of crushed red pepper for extra spice if desired
- Keep the dip cool until serving to maintain freshness

Nutritional Values: Calories: 98, Fat: 2g, Carbs: 14g, Protein: 8g, Sugar: 7g, Sodium: 160 mg, Potassium: 320 mg, Cholesterol: 5 mg

2. APPETIZERS FOR ENTERTAINING

HERBED GOAT CHEESE STUFFED CHERRY TOMATOES

Preparation Time: 15 min
Cooking Time: none
Mode of Cooking: No Cooking
Servings: 12

Ingredients:

- 24 cherry tomatoes
- 4 oz goat cheese, softened
- 1 Tbsp fresh basil, finely chopped
- 1 Tbsp fresh chives, finely chopped
- 1 Tbsp fresh parsley, finely chopped
- 1 clove garlic, minced
- Zest of 1 lemon
- Salt and pepper to taste

Directions:

1. Slice the tops off the cherry tomatoes and scoop out the insides to create a hollow shell
2. In a mixing bowl, combine goat cheese, basil, chives, parsley, garlic, and lemon zest
3. Season the mixture with salt and pepper
4. Fill each cherry tomato with the goat cheese mixture using a small spoon or a piping bag

Tips:

- For added flavor, let the stuffed tomatoes chill for about an hour before serving
- Use a melon baller to easily scoop out the insides of the tomatoes without breaking them

Nutritional Values: Calories: 50, Fat: 4g, Carbs: 1g, Protein: 3g, Sugar: 1g, Sodium: 30 mg, Potassium: 90 mg, Cholesterol: 5 mg

MEDITERRANEAN TUNA STUFFED CHERRY TOMATOES

Preparation Time: 20 min
Cooking Time: none
Mode of Cooking: No Cooking
Servings: 15
Ingredients:

- 30 cherry tomatoes
- 1 can (5 oz) tuna in water, drained
- 2 Tbsp Kalamata olives, pitted and finely chopped
- 1 Tbsp capers, rinsed and chopped
- 2 Tbsp red onion, finely chopped
- 1 tsp Dijon mustard
- 1 Tbsp extra-virgin olive oil
- 1 Tbsp fresh parsley, chopped
- Salt and pepper to taste

Directions:

1. Slice the tops off the cherry tomatoes and remove the insides
2. In a bowl, mix together tuna, olives, capers, onion, mustard, olive oil, and parsley
3. Season with salt and pepper to taste
4. Stuff this mixture into the hollowed-out cherry tomatoes

Tips:

- Chilling the stuffed tomatoes enhances the flavor making them perfect as a make-ahead appetizer
- Use a small teaspoon to fill the tomatoes easily without spoiling their shape

Nutritional Values: Calories: 30, Fat: 1g, Carbs: 1g, Protein: 4g, Sugar: 0g, Sodium: 45 mg, Potassium: 60 mg, Cholesterol: 5 mg

CUCUMBER FETA STUFFED CHERRY TOMATOES

Preparation Time: 10 min
Cooking Time: none
Mode of Cooking: No Cooking
Servings: 10
Ingredients:

- 20 cherry tomatoes
- 1/2 cup crumbled feta cheese
- 1/4 cup cucumber, finely diced
- 1 Tbsp dill, chopped
- 1 tsp lemon juice
- Black pepper to taste

Directions:

1. Cut a small slice from the bottom of each cherry tomato so they stand upright
2. Cut off the top and gently scoop out the insides

3. In a small bowl, mix feta, cucumber, dill, and lemon juice
4. Season with black pepper
5. Spoon or pipe the filling into the tomatoes

Tips:
- Serve immediately or keep chilled until serving for better flavor integration
- Pair with a sparkling mineral water for a refreshing appetizer experience

Nutritional Values: Calories: 20, Fat: 1g, Carbs: 1g, Protein: 1g, Sugar: 1g, Sodium: 25 mg, Potassium: 30 mg, Cholesterol: 5 mg

CREAMY SPINACH AND ARTICHOKE DIP

Preparation Time: 15 min
Cooking Time: 20 min
Mode of Cooking: Baking
Servings: 8
Ingredients:

- 1 C. fresh spinach, finely chopped
- 1 C. canned artichoke hearts, drained and chopped
- 1 C. low-fat Greek yogurt
- 1/2 C. low-fat cream cheese, softened
- 1/4 C. Parmesan cheese, grated
- 2 cloves garlic, minced
- 1 tsp onion powder
- 1/2 tsp black pepper
- 1/4 tsp salt

Directions:

1. Preheat oven to 375°F (190°C)
2. In a large mixing bowl, combine spinach, artichoke hearts, Greek yogurt, cream cheese, Parmesan cheese, garlic, onion powder, black pepper, and salt until well mixed
3. Transfer the mixture to a baking dish and smooth the top
4. Bake in the preheated oven until bubbly and slightly golden, about 20 minutes

Tips:
- Serve warm with whole-grain crackers for added fiber
- Add a dash of red pepper flakes for a spicy twist
- Garnish with chopped chives for added color and flavor

Nutritional Values: Calories: 98, Fat: 4g, Carbs: 9g, Protein: 7g, Sugar: 3g, Sodium: 216 mg, Potassium: 211 mg, Cholesterol: 11 mg

ZESTY LIME SPINACH ARTICHOKE DIP

Preparation Time: 10 min
Cooking Time: none
Mode of Cooking: Mixing
Servings: 6
Ingredients:

- 1 C. fresh spinach, chopped
- 1 C. artichoke hearts, drained and chopped
- 1/2 C. avocado, mashed
- 1/4 C. sour cream, low-fat
- Juice of 1 lime
- 1 Tbsp fresh cilantro, chopped
- 1/4 tsp chili powder
- Salt and pepper to taste

Directions:

1. In a bowl, combine chopped spinach, chopped artichoke hearts, mashed avocado, low-fat sour cream, lime juice, cilantro, chili powder, salt, and pepper until well combined
2. Chill the mixture in the refrigerator for at least 30 minutes to blend the flavors

Tips:
- Serve chilled for a refreshing summer dip
- Pair with homemade pita chips for a healthier option
- Enhance the dip's texture with a sprinkle of toasted sesame seeds on top before serving

Nutritional Values: Calories: 85, Fat: 6g, Carbs: 7g, Protein: 2g, Sugar: 1g, Sodium: 95 mg, Potassium: 175 mg, Cholesterol: 5 mg

MEDITERRANEAN SPINACH AND ARTICHOKE HUMMUS DIP

Preparation Time: 12 min
Cooking Time: none
Mode of Cooking: Blending
Servings: 8
Ingredients:

- 1 C. cooked chickpeas
- 1/2 C. fresh spinach
- 1/2 C. artichoke hearts, drained and chopped
- 1/4 C. tahini
- 2 Tbsp olive oil
- 1 Tbsp lemon juice
- 1 clove garlic, minced
- 1 tsp ground cumin
- Salt to taste

Directions:

1. In a food processor, blend chickpeas, spinach, artichoke hearts, tahini, olive oil, lemon juice, garlic, and cumin until smooth
2. Season with salt to taste
3. Transfer to a serving bowl and drizzle with a little extra olive oil

Tips:

- Drizzle with pomegranate molasses for a sweet touch
- Serve with vegetable sticks such as carrots and cucumbers for a wholesome snack
- Top with a pinch of paprika for a pop of color and flavor

Nutritional Values: Calories: 130, Fat: 9g, Carbs: 11g, Protein: 4g, Sugar: 2g, Sodium: 120 mg, Potassium: 189 mg, Cholesterol: 0 mg

MINI CAPRESE SKEWERS

Preparation Time: 15 min
Cooking Time: none
Mode of Cooking: No Cooking
Servings: 20
Ingredients:

- 20 small mozzarella balls
- 20 fresh basil leaves
- 20 cherry tomatoes
- 2 Tbsp extra virgin olive oil
- 1 Tbsp balsamic glaze
- Salt to taste
- Freshly ground black pepper to taste

Directions:

1. Thread mozzarella, basil, and a cherry tomato onto each skewer
2. Arrange on a plate
3. Drizzle with olive oil and balsamic glaze
4. Sprinkle lightly with salt and freshly ground black pepper

Tips:

- Serve immediately or cover and refrigerate until serving
- Use toothpicks for a more delicate presentation
- Pair with a sparkling mineral water for a refreshing combo

Nutritional Values: Calories: 45, Fat: 3.5g, Carbs: 1g, Protein: 2.5g, Sugar: 1g, Sodium: 20 mg, Potassium: 15 mg, Cholesterol: 10 mg

SMOKED SALMON CAPRESE BITES

Preparation Time: 20 min
Cooking Time: none
Mode of Cooking: No Cooking
Servings: 15
Ingredients:

- 15 cucumber slices, about 1/2 inch thick
- 15 smoked salmon strips, small
- 15 mini mozzarella balls
- 15 small dill sprigs
- 1 Tbsp capers
- 1 Tbsp extra virgin olive oil

- Lemon zest for garnish

Directions:

1. Place cucumber slices on a serving platter
2. Top each slice with a mozzarella ball, a twist of smoked salmon, and a dill sprig
3. Garnish each with a few capers and lemon zest
4. Drizzle with olive oil just before serving

Tips:

- Chill before serving to enhance the flavors
- Opt for wild-caught salmon for higher omega-3 content
- Lemon zest adds a fresh, zesty kick enhancing the overall flavor

Nutritional Values: Calories: 50, Fat: 3.8g, Carbs: 1g, Protein: 3.5g, Sugar: 0.5g, Sodium: 200 mg, Potassium: 30 mg, Cholesterol: 15 mg

PESTO-STUFFED CHERRY TOMATOES

Preparation Time: 30 min
Cooking Time: none
Mode of Cooking: No Cooking
Servings: 30
Ingredients:

- 30 cherry tomatoes
- 1/2 cup basil pesto
- 1/4 cup pine nuts, toasted
- Grated Parmesan cheese for topping

Directions:

1. Slice the tops off the cherry tomatoes and scoop out the insides
2. Fill each tomato with basil pesto
3. Sprinkle toasted pine nuts and grated Parmesan on top

Tips:

- Serve chilled or at room temperature
- Top with a drizzle of aged balsamic vinegar for an extra flavor boost

- Can be made a day ahead and stored in the refrigerator

Nutritional Values: Calories: 35, Fat: 2.5g, Carbs: 2g, Protein: 1g, Sugar: 1g, Sodium: 45 mg, Potassium: 40 mg, Cholesterol: 2 mg

3. QUICK BITES

ZESTY LEMON HERB GREEK YOGURT DIP

Preparation Time: 5 min
Cooking Time: none
Mode of Cooking: No cooking
Servings: 4
Ingredients:

- 1 cup plain Greek yogurt
- 2 Tbsp fresh lemon juice
- 1 Tbsp chopped fresh dill
- 1 Tbsp chopped fresh parsley
- 1 clove garlic, minced
- ¼ tsp black pepper
- ¼ tsp salt (optional)

Directions:

1. Combine Greek yogurt, lemon juice, dill, parsley, minced garlic, black pepper, and salt in a bowl
2. Stir thoroughly until all ingredients are well distributed
3. Chill in the refrigerator before serving

Tips:

- Serve with fresh vegetables for a healthful snack
- Use as a dressing for summer salads
- Adjust herbs according to season for variation

Nutritional Values: Calories: 45, Fat: 1g, Carbs: 3g, Protein: 6g, Sugar: 2g, Sodium: 55 mg, Potassium: 60 mg, Cholesterol: 5 mg

Spicy Roasted Red Pepper and Yogurt Dip

Preparation Time: 10 min
Cooking Time: none
Mode of Cooking: No cooking
Servings: 4
Ingredients:

- 1 cup plain Greek yogurt
- 1 roasted red pepper, skin removed and chopped
- 1 tsp smoked paprika
- ½ tsp crushed red pepper flakes
- 1 clove garlic, minced
- 1 Tbsp olive oil
- ¼ tsp salt (optional)

Directions:

1. Combine Greek yogurt, chopped roasted red pepper, smoked paprika, red pepper flakes, minced garlic, and olive oil in a mixing bowl
2. Mix the ingredients until the dip is smooth and even in texture
3. Chill in the refrigerator to enhance the flavors

Tips:

- Serve with whole-grain pita chips or fresh cut veggies
- Stir in a tablespoon of chopped basil for an Italian twist
- Add more red pepper flakes if you prefer a hotter dip

Nutritional Values: Calories: 70, Fat: 5g, Carbs: 4g, Protein: 4g, Sugar: 3g, Sodium: 60 mg, Potassium: 50 mg, Cholesterol: 5 mg

Cucumber Mint Greek Yogurt Dip

Preparation Time: 7 min
Cooking Time: none
Mode of Cooking: No cooking
Servings: 4
Ingredients:

- 1 cup plain Greek Yogurt
- ½ cucumber, grated and water squeezed out
- 2 Tbsp chopped fresh mint
- 1 Tbsp lemon juice
- 1 clove garlic, minced
- ¼ tsp salt (optional)
- ⅛ tsp black pepper

Directions:

1. Combine Greek yogurt, grated cucumber, fresh mint, lemon juice, minced garlic, salt, and black pepper in a bowl
2. Stir to blend all the ingredients evenly
3. Chill for at least 30 minutes before serving to allow flavors to meld

Tips:

- Pair with toasted flatbread for a refreshing snack
- Squeeze additional lemon juice on top before serving for extra zest
- Mix in a teaspoon of chopped dill for additional herb flavor

Nutritional Values: Calories: 50, Fat: 1g, Carbs: 3g, Protein: 6g, Sugar: 2g, Sodium: 65 mg, Potassium: 88 mg, Cholesterol: 5 mg

Tropical Cottage Cheese Delight

Preparation Time: 5 min
Cooking Time: none
Mode of Cooking: No Cooking
Servings: 1
Ingredients:

- ½ cup low-fat cottage cheese
- ½ cup chopped pineapple
- 2 Tbsp sliced almonds
- 1 Tbsp honey
- 1 tsp chia seeds

Directions:

1. Combine cottage cheese and pineapple in a bowl
2. Top with sliced almonds and chia seeds
3. Drizzle honey over the top

Tips:

- Serve immediately for best flavor
- Can substitute pineapple with mango for a different taste

Nutritional Values: Calories: 200, Fat: 4g, Carbs: 30g, Protein: 12g, Sugar: 20g, Sodium: 200 mg, Potassium: 150 mg, Cholesterol: 5 mg

PINEAPPLE COTTAGE CHEESE SALSA

Preparation Time: 10 min
Cooking Time: none
Mode of Cooking: No Cooking
Servings: 2
Ingredients:

- 1 cup diced pineapple
- 1 cup low-fat cottage cheese
- ¼ cup diced red bell pepper
- ¼ cup diced cucumber
- 2 Tbsp finely chopped jalapeno
- 2 Tbsp lime juice
- 1 Tbsp cilantro, chopped
- Salt to taste

Directions:

1. Mix all ingredients in a bowl until combined
2. Chill in the refrigerator for at least 30 minutes before serving

Tips:

- Great as a dip with whole-grain tortilla chips
- Adjust lime juice and jalapeno according to taste preference

Nutritional Values: Calories: 90, Fat: 1g, Carbs: 12g, Protein: 9g, Sugar: 8g, Sodium: 180 mg, Potassium: 120 mg, Cholesterol: 5 mg

COTTAGE CHEESE PINEAPPLE RINGS

Preparation Time: 15 min
Cooking Time: none
Mode of Cooking: No Cooking
Servings: 4
Ingredients:

- 4 pineapple rings
- 1 cup low-fat cottage cheese
- 4 tsp honey
- ½ tsp ground cinnamon
- Mint leaves for garnish

Directions:

1. Place pineapple rings on serving plates
2. Fill the center of each ring with cottage cheese
3. Drizzle honey and sprinkle cinnamon over the cottage cheese

Tips:

- Garnish with mint leaves before serving
- Can be served as a refreshing dessert or a sweet snack

Nutritional Values: Calories: 100, Fat: 1g, Carbs: 15g, Protein: 7g, Sugar: 12g, Sodium: 80 mg, Potassium: 90 mg, Cholesterol: 3 mg

HONEY CINNAMON ROASTED CHICKPEAS

Preparation Time: 10 min
Cooking Time: 30 min
Mode of Cooking: Oven
Servings: 3
Ingredients:

- 2 cups chickpeas, rinsed and dried
- 1 Tbsp coconut oil, melted
- 2 Tbsp honey
- 1 tsp ground cinnamon

Directions:

1. Preheat oven to 350°F (177°C)
2. Combine honey, cinnamon, and coconut oil in a bowl
3. Add chickpeas and toss to coat thoroughly
4. Spread chickpeas on a lined baking sheet and bake for 30 minutes, stirring occasionally, until golden brown

Tips:
- Mix with dried cranberries post-cooking for a sweet twist
- Cool completely before serving to enhance texture

Nutritional Values: Calories: 195, Fat: 6g, Carbs: 31g, Protein: 5g, Sugar: 11g, Sodium: 55mg, Potassium: 274 mg, Cholesterol: 0 mg

GARLIC PARMESAN ROASTED CHICKPEAS

Preparation Time: 10 min
Cooking Time: 22 min
Mode of Cooking: Oven
Servings: 4
Ingredients:

- 2 cups chickpeas, drained and dried
- 1 Tbsp olive oil
- 1 tsp garlic powder
- 1/4 cup grated Parmesan cheese
- 1/2 tsp black pepper

Directions:

1. Preheat oven to 400°F (204°C)
2. Toss chickpeas with olive oil, garlic powder, black pepper, and half the Parmesan
3. Spread on a baking tray and roast for 22 minutes
4. Sprinkle remaining Parmesan over hot chickpeas and serve

Tips:
- Serve as a topping over salads or soups for added crunch
- Store in a cool, dry place for up to a week

Nutritional Values: Calories: 160, Fat: 7g, Carbs: 18g, Protein: 7g, Sugar: 3g, Sodium: 110mg, Potassium: 290 mg, Cholesterol: 4 mg

SPICY TURMERIC ROASTED CHICKPEAS

Preparation Time: 12 min
Cooking Time: 20 min
Mode of Cooking: Oven
Servings: 3
Ingredients:

- 2 cups chickpeas, well-dried
- 1 Tbsp coconut oil
- 1 tsp turmeric powder
- 1/2 tsp cayenne pepper
- 1/2 tsp sea salt

Directions:

1. Preheat oven to 375°F (190°C)
2. Mix chickpeas with coconut oil, turmeric, cayenne, and sea salt until well covered
3. Spread them on a parchment-lined sheet and bake for 20 minutes, shaking the pan halfway through for even roasting

Tips:
- Sprinkle with lime zest for a zesty kick
- Can be enjoyed alone or as a salad topper

Nutritional Values: Calories: 180, Fat: 6g, Carbs: 24g, Protein: 6g, Sugar: 0g, Sodium: 200mg, Potassium: 332 mg, Cholesterol: 0 mg

CHAPTER 10: DESSERTS AND TREATS

Who says heart-healthy eating means skipping the sweet stuff? Not here in Chapter 10, where we celebrate the joy of desserts and treats while faithfully adhering to the principles of the DASH diet. It's about striking a balance, indulging your sweet tooth responsibly, and embracing delicious, nutritious options that align with your health goals.

Consider this: the satisfying conclusion to a day of balanced eating doesn't have to be devoid of pleasure. In fact, as we explore a plethora of divine yet simple desserts, you'll discover how natural ingredients and mindful preparation can transform the way you think about sweets.

Imagine biting into a juicy, spice-infused baked apple, or savoring a chilled berry parfait layered with lush, low-fat yogurt. These aren't just treats; they're testaments to the fact that desserts can be both wholesome and indulgent. By wisely choosing ingredients that add health benefits—like fruits rich in antioxidants, nuts packed with heart-healthy fats, and spices that naturally enhance flavor without the need for excess sugar—we create desserts that not only please the palate but also nourish the body.

But the sweetness doesn't stop there. Alongside our fruit-focused desserts, we delve into innovative low-sodium sweet treats that offer the creamy, dreamy textures you crave, minus the health risks associated with too much salt. And for those warm days or special occasions, our section on refreshing beverages will show you how to whip up smoothies, iced teas, and other drinks that are both hydrating and delightfully tasty.

Here in our dessert chapter, it's all about celebrating the naturally sweet and the subtly indulgent. Whether you're rounding off a family meal, hosting a gathering, or simply treating yourself, these recipes ensure that you can relax, enjoy, and still stay true to your healthful eating commitments. So, let's turn up the flavor and turn down the guilt as we explore the sweetest part of living healthily. Ready to treat yourself? Let's indulge—wisely, of course!

1. FRUIT-BASED DESSERTS

CINNAMON SPICE BAKED APPLES

Preparation Time: 15 min
Cooking Time: 45 min
Mode of Cooking: Baking
Servings: 4

Ingredients:

- 4 large tart apples, cored
- 4 tsp unsalted butter
- 1/4 cup brown sugar, packed
- 1/2 tsp ground cinnamon
- 1/4 tsp ground nutmeg
- 1/4 cup chopped walnuts
- 1/4 cup raisins
- 1/2 cup apple juice

Directions:

1. Preheat oven to 375°F (190°C)
2. Place apples in a baking dish
3. Mix brown sugar, cinnamon, nutmeg, and fill each apple with this mixture
4. Top each with a teaspoon of butter
5. Pour apple juice around the apples in the dish

6. Bake in preheated oven until apples are soft and filling is bubbly, about 45 min

Tips:

- Serve warm with low-fat vanilla yogurt for a creamy addition
- Store leftovers in the refrigerator and reheat before serving

Nutritional Values: Calories: 210, Fat: 4g, Carbs: 43g, Protein: 1g, Sugar: 36g, Sodium: 5mg, Potassium: 195mg, Cholesterol: 10mg

MAPLE GINGER BAKED APPLES

Preparation Time: 10 min
Cooking Time: 1 hr
Mode of Cooking: Baking
Servings: 4
Ingredients:

- 4 large sweet apples, cored
- 1/4 cup maple syrup
- 1 Tbsp fresh ginger, grated
- 2 Tbsp unsalted butter, melted
- 1/3 cup dried cranberries
- 1/3 cup chopped pecans
- 1/2 tsp ground allspice
- 3/4 cup water

Directions:

1. Preheat oven to 350°F (175°C)
2. Place apples in a baking dish
3. Combine maple syrup, melted butter, ginger, and allspice in a bowl
4. Stir in cranberries and pecans
5. Spoon the mixture into the center of each apple
6. Add water to the baking dish
7. Bake until the apples are tender and the stuffing is heated through, about 1 hr

Tips:

- Accompany with a sprinkle of ground cloves for extra spice
- Ideal paired with a dollop of Greek yogurt

Nutritional Values: Calories: 255, Fat: 11g, Carbs: 41g, Protein: 1g, Sugar: 30g, Sodium: 10mg, Potassium: 220mg, Cholesterol: 15mg

ALMOND CRUNCH BAKED APPLES

Preparation Time: 20 min
Cooking Time: 40 min
Mode of Cooking: Baking
Servings: 6
Ingredients:

- 6 medium apples, cored
- 1/2 cup rolled oats
- 1/3 cup sliced almonds
- 1/4 cup honey
- 2 Tbsp unsalted butter, melted
- 1 tsp vanilla extract
- 1/2 tsp ground cardamom
- 1/2 cup orange juice

Directions:

1. Preheat oven to 375°F (190°C)
2. In a bowl, combine oats, almonds, melted butter, honey, vanilla, and cardamom
3. Fill apples with the oat mixture
4. Pour orange juice into the baking dish around the apples
5. Bake until apples are soft and topping is golden, about 40 min

Tips:

- For extra crunch top with more almonds before serving
- A drizzle of caramel sauce can add a delightful twist

Nutritional Values: Calories: 210, Fat: 7g, Carbs: 37g, Protein: 3g, Sugar: 27g, Sodium: 5mg, Potassium: 250mg, Cholesterol: 10mg

MIXED BERRY AND CHIA PARFAIT

Preparation Time: 15 min
Cooking Time: none

Mode of Cooking: No Cooking
Servings: 2
Ingredients:

- 1 cup Greek yogurt, unsweetened
- 2 Tbsp chia seeds
- 1 Tbsp honey
- ½ cup blueberries
- ½ cup raspberries
- ½ cup strawberries, sliced
- 4 Tbsp almond slivers, toasted

Directions:

1. Stir honey and chia seeds into Greek yogurt and let sit for 10 min to thicken
2. Layer the thickened yogurt mixture with blueberries, raspberries, and strawberries in two serving glasses
3. Garnish with toasted almond slivers

Tips:

- Mix berries of your choice to add variety
- Place in the refrigerator overnight for a thicker texture

Nutritional Values: Calories: 295, Fat: 15g, Carbs: 34g, Protein: 12g, Sugar: 20g, Sodium: 60 mg, Potassium: 400 mg, Cholesterol: 10 mg

POMEGRANATE PISTACHIO GREEK YOGURT PARFAIT

Preparation Time: 10 min
Cooking Time: none
Mode of Cooking: No Cooking
Servings: 2
Ingredients:

- 1 cup Greek yogurt, unsweetened
- 1 Tbsp pomegranate molasses
- ½ cup pomegranate seeds
- ½ cup granola, low-fat
- 2 Tbsp shelled pistachios, chopped

Directions:

1. Combine Greek yogurt with pomegranate molasses
2. Spoon half of the yogurt into two glasses, following with a layer of pomegranate seeds and granola
3. Repeat the layers and top with chopped pistachios

Tips:

- Serve immediately or chill to allow the flavors to meld
- Using homemade granola can reduce sugar and sodium content

Nutritional Values: Calories: 310, Fat: 10g, Carbs: 42g, Protein: 15g, Sugar: 25g, Sodium: 85 mg, Potassium: 360 mg, Cholesterol: 5 mg

KIWI LIME GREEK YOGURT PARFAIT

Preparation Time: 10 min
Cooking Time: none
Mode of Cooking: No Cooking
Servings: 2
Ingredients:

- 1 cup Greek yogurt, unsweetened
- 1 tsp lime zest
- 2 kiwis, peeled and diced
- ½ cup granola, low-fat
- 1 Tbsp honey
- 2 tsp lime juice

Directions:

1. Mix Greek yogurt with lime zest, honey, and lime juice
2. Layer yogurt mixture, diced kiwi, and granola alternately in two serving bowls

Tips:

- Opt for organic honey for better flavor
- This parfait is ideal as a refreshing breakfast or dessert

Nutritional Values: Calories: 270, Fat: 8g, Carbs: 38g, Protein: 13g, Sugar: 22g, Sodium: 55 mg, Potassium: 410 mg, Cholesterol: 10 mg

GRILLED PEACHES WITH HONEY AND THYME

Preparation Time: 10 min.
Cooking Time: 6 min.
Mode of Cooking: Grilling
Servings: 4
Ingredients:

- 4 large peaches, halved and pitted
- 1 tbsp olive oil
- 4 tbsp honey
- 1 tsp fresh thyme, chopped
- ½ tsp ground cinnamon
- ¼ tsp salt

Directions:

1. Preheat grill to medium-high heat (about 375°F or 190°C)
2. Brush peach halves with olive oil
3. Place on the grill cut side down and grill for 3 min.
4. Turn peaches over, drizzle with honey, sprinkle with cinnamon, thyme, and salt, grill for another 3 min.

Tips:

- Serve immediately with a dollop of Greek yogurt if desired
- Adding a spritz of lemon juice can enhance the peaches' natural tartness
- Pair with a light white wine for an elegant dessert option

Nutritional Values: Calories: 110, Fat: 2.5g, Carbs: 25g, Protein: 1g, Sugar: 21g, Sodium: 150 mg, Potassium: 285 mg, Cholesterol: 0 mg

GRILLED PEACH AND RICOTTA CROSTINI

Preparation Time: 15 min.
Cooking Time: 8 min.
Mode of Cooking: Grilling
Servings: 6
Ingredients:

- 6 slices of whole-grain baguette
- 1 cup ricotta cheese
- 3 large peaches, sliced
- 2 tbsp honey
- 1 tbsp olive oil
- Fresh basil leaves, chopped
- Black pepper
- Flake sea salt

Directions:

1. Preheat grill to medium heat (350°F or 177°C)
2. Brush peach slices and baguette slices with olive oil
3. Grill peaches and baguette slices for about 4 min. on each side until golden
4. Spread ricotta on each baguette slice, top with grilled peach slices, drizzle with honey, and garnish with basil, black pepper, and sea salt

Tips:

- A hint of balsamic reduction can add a zesty twist
- Use almond ricotta for a dairy-free alternative
- Perfect as an appetizer or light dessert

Nutritional Values: Calories: 180, Fat: 9g, Carbs: 20g, Protein: 6g, Sugar: 9g, Sodium: 190 mg, Potassium: 150 mg, Cholesterol: 15 mg

PEACHES GRILLED WITH VANILLA AND GINGER

Preparation Time: 12 min.
Cooking Time: 5 min.
Mode of Cooking: Grilling
Servings: 4
Ingredients:

- 4 large ripe peaches, halved and pitted
- 2 tbsp brown sugar
- 1 tsp ground ginger
- 1 vanilla bean, split and seeds scraped
- 4 tsp unsalted butter, cut into small pieces
- Mint leaves for garnish

Directions:

1. Preheat a grill to high (400°F or 204°C)
2. Mix ginger, vanilla bean seeds, and brown sugar in a small bowl
3. Place a piece of butter in the cavity of each peach half, sprinkle sugar mixture
4. Grill peaches cut side down for 2-3 min.
5. Flip and grill for another 2 min.

Tips:

- Garnish with fresh mint leaves just before serving
- Serve with a scoop of low-fat vanilla ice cream or frozen yogurt for extra indulgence
- Vanilla pod can be replaced with a splash of pure vanilla extract for convenience

Nutritional Values: Calories: 120, Fat: 4g, Carbs: 20g, Protein: 1g, Sugar: 18g, Sodium: 5 mg, Potassium: 190 mg, Cholesterol: 10 mg

2. Low-Sodium Sweet Treats

Cherry Pistachio Dark Chocolate Bark

Preparation Time: 15 min
Cooking Time: 30 min
Mode of Cooking: Refrigeration
Servings: 8
Ingredients:

- 8 oz. dark chocolate, at least 70% cacao, coarsely chopped
- 1/4 cup dried cherries, chopped
- 1/4 cup unsalted pistachios, chopped
- 1/4 tsp sea salt, finely ground

Directions:

1. Melt dark chocolate in a double boiler over simmering water until smooth, stirring frequently
2. Pour melted chocolate onto a parchment-lined baking tray, spreading to form an even layer
3. Sprinkle chopped cherries and pistachios evenly over the chocolate
4. Lightly press the toppings into the chocolate; sprinkle sea salt evenly over the surface
5. Refrigerate until set, approximately 30 min
6. Break into pieces

Tips:

- Store in an airtight container in a cool, dry place to maintain freshness
- Serving immediately after setting enhances the crispiness and flavor

Nutritional Values: Calories: 180, Fat: 12g, Carbs: 15g, Protein: 2g, Sugar: 8g, Sodium: 60mg, Potassium: 210mg, Cholesterol: 1mg

Minty Orange Peel Dark Chocolate Bark

Preparation Time: 20 min
Cooking Time: 30 min
Mode of Cooking: Refrigeration
Servings: 10
Ingredients:

- 8 oz. dark chocolate, at least 70% cacao, broken into pieces
- 1/4 cup candied orange peel, thinly sliced
- 1 tbsp fresh mint, finely chopped
- 1/8 tsp fleur de sel

Directions:

1. Melt dark chocolate pieces in a microwave-safe bowl in 30-second intervals, stirring between each, until fully melted
2. Mix half the candied orange peel and mint into melted chocolate
3. Pour the chocolate mixture onto a parchment-lined tray and spread evenly
4. Sprinkle the remaining orange peel and mint on top
5. Dust with fleur de sel
6. Refrigerate until firm, about 30 min
7. Break into shards

Tips:

- Do not overheat the chocolate; microwave in short bursts to prevent burning
- Chocolate can be tempered for a shinier finish and a crisper snap
- Fresh mint can be substituted with a drop of peppermint extract for a stronger mint flavor

Nutritional Values: Calories: 190, Fat: 11g, Carbs: 20g, Protein: 2g, Sugar: 15g, Sodium: 25mg, Potassium: 220mg, Cholesterol: 0mg

ROSEMARY HAZELNUT DARK CHOCOLATE BARK

Preparation Time: 10 min
Cooking Time: 2 hr
Mode of Cooking: Freezing
Servings: 8
Ingredients:

- 8 oz. dark chocolate, at least 70% cacao, finely chopped
- 1/4 cup roasted hazelnuts, coarsely chopped
- 2 tsp fresh rosemary, finely chopped
- 1/4 tsp Himalayan pink salt

Directions:

1. Temper dark chocolate by heating three-quarters in a heatproof bowl over a pot of simmering water until chocolate reaches 115°F (46°C), then remove from heat and add the remaining chocolate, stirring until melted
2. Spread the chocolate on a parchment-lined baking sheet
3. Sprinkle with chopped hazelnuts and rosemary, pressing them slightly into the chocolate
4. Finish with a sprinkle of pink salt
5. Freeze until solid, about 2 hr
6. Break into rustic pieces

Tips:

- If hazelnuts are raw, toast them lightly in a dry skillet for enhanced flavor
- Breaking the bark into irregular pieces adds a homemade touch
- Rosemary should be used sparingly to avoid overpowering the other flavors

Nutritional Values: Calories: 175, Fat: 13g, Carbs: 13g, Protein: 2g, Sugar: 10g, Sodium: 30mg, Potassium: 200mg, Cholesterol: 0mg

CLASSIC LOW-SODIUM OATMEAL RAISIN COOKIES

Preparation Time: 15 min.
Cooking Time: 12 min.
Mode of Cooking: Baking
Servings: 24
Ingredients:

- 1 C. rolled oats
- 1/2 C. whole wheat flour
- 1/4 C. raisins
- 1/2 tsp baking soda
- 1/4 C. unsalted butter, softened
- 1/4 C. apple sauce
- 1/2 C. erythritol
- 1 large egg
- 1 tsp vanilla extract
- 1/2 tsp cinnamon

Directions:

1. Preheat oven to 350°F (175°C)
2. In a large bowl, cream together butter, apple sauce, and erythritol until smooth
3. Beat in egg and vanilla
4. Combine oats, whole wheat flour, baking soda, and cinnamon in another bowl
5. Gradually add dry ingredients to wet ingredients
6. Stir in raisins
7. Drop dough by spoonfuls onto ungreased baking sheets
8. Bake for 12 min. or until edges start to brown

Tips:

- Use parchment paper for easier cleanup

- Store cookies in an airtight container to retain softness

Nutritional Values: Calories: 90, Fat: 3g, Carbs: 15g, Protein: 2g, Sugar: 5g, Sodium: 20 mg, Potassium: 75 mg, Cholesterol: 15 mg

ALMOND OATMEAL COOKIES WITH DATE PURÉE

Preparation Time: 20 min.
Cooking Time: 14 min.
Mode of Cooking: Baking
Servings: 20
Ingredients:

- 1 C. rolled oats
- 1/3 C. almond meal
- 1/4 C. date puree
- 1/4 tsp baking soda
- 1/4 tsp salt substitute
- 1/4 C. unsalted almond butter
- 1/3 C. coconut sugar
- 1 large egg
- 1 tsp almond extract
- 1/4 C. chopped almonds
- 1/4 C. raisins

Directions:

1. Preheat oven to 375°F (190°C)
2. In a mixing bowl, blend almond butter, date puree, and coconut sugar until creamy
3. Add egg and almond extract, mix well
4. Combine rolled oats, almond meal, baking soda, and salt substitute in separate bowl
5. Gradually mix dry ingredients into wet ingredients
6. Fold in chopped almonds and raisins
7. Drop dough by spoonfuls onto lined baking sheets
8. Bake for 14 min.

Tips:

- Chill dough for 10 min. before baking to prevent spreading

- Substitute raisins with dried cranberries for a tart twist

Nutritional Values: Calories: 110, Fat: 5g, Carbs: 15g, Protein: 3g, Sugar: 8g, Sodium: 15 mg, Potassium: 85 mg, Cholesterol: 20 mg

OATMEAL SPICE COOKIES

Preparation Time: 18 min.
Cooking Time: 15 min.
Mode of Cooking: Baking
Servings: 25
Ingredients:

- 1 C. rolled oats
- 1/4 C. whole wheat flour
- 1/4 tsp baking powder
- 1/4 tsp ground nutmeg
- 1/4 tsp ground cloves
- 1/2 C. unsalted butter, softened
- 1/2 C. monk fruit sweetener
- 1 egg
- 1 tsp vanilla extract
- 1/2 C. raisins
- 1/4 C. chopped walnuts

Directions:

1. Preheat oven to 375°F (190°C)
2. Cream butter and monk fruit sweetener until light
3. Beat in egg and vanilla
4. Mix together oats, flour, baking powder, nutmeg, and cloves in another bowl
5. Gradually add dry mix to wet, stir until combined
6. Stir in raisins and walnuts
7. Spoon dough onto parchment-lined baking sheets
8. Bake for 15 min. or until golden

Tips:

- Toast walnuts before adding to dough for enhanced flavor

- Store cookies in a cool, dry place to maintain freshness

Nutritional Values: Calories: 80, Fat: 4g, Carbs: 11g, Protein: 2g, Sugar: 2g, Sodium: 10 mg, Potassium: 90 mg, Cholesterol: 10 mg

CLASSIC VANILLA CHIA SEED PUDDING

Preparation Time: 10 min
Cooking Time: none
Mode of Cooking: No Cooking
Servings: 2
Ingredients:

- 1 cup unsweetened almond milk
- 3 Tbsp chia seeds
- 1 tsp vanilla extract
- 1 Tbsp maple syrup
- Fresh berries for topping
- Mint leaves for garnish

Directions:

1. Combine almond milk, chia seeds, vanilla extract, and maple syrup in a bowl
2. Stir thoroughly until the mixture is well combined
3. Cover and refrigerate overnight to allow the chia seeds to swell and absorb the liquid
4. Serve chilled, topped with fresh berries and mint leaves for garnish

Tips:

- Stir the mixture a few times within the first hour to prevent clumping and ensure even gel formation
- Customize with a sprinkle of cinnamon or a dash of nutmeg for a spicy twist

Nutritional Values: Calories: 180, Fat: 9g, Carbs: 20g, Protein: 5g, Sugar: 8g, Sodium: 30 mg, Potassium: 150 mg, Cholesterol: 0 mg

CHOCOLATE HAZELNUT CHIA PUDDING

Preparation Time: 15 min
Cooking Time: none
Mode of Cooking: No Cooking
Servings: 2
Ingredients:

- 1 cup unsweetened coconut milk
- 3 Tbsp chia seeds
- 2 Tbsp cocoa powder
- 1 Tbsp hazelnut butter
- 1 tsp pure vanilla extract
- 1 Tbsp honey or agave syrup

Directions:

1. In a mixing bowl, combine coconut milk, chia seeds, cocoa powder, hazelnut butter, vanilla extract, and honey
2. Mix until the cocoa powder is fully incorporated and the mixture is smooth
3. Cover and let sit in the refrigerator overnight
4. Serve chilled, optionally topped with crushed hazelnuts and a drizzle of hazelnut butter

Tips:

- Mix well to ensure the cocoa powder does not form clumps
- Add a pinch of sea salt to enhance the chocolate flavor
- If a thinner consistency is preferred, add an extra splash of coconut milk before serving

Nutritional Values: Calories: 195, Fat: 12g, Carbs: 21g, Protein: 4g, Sugar: 11g, Sodium: 35 mg, Potassium: 200 mg, Cholesterol: 0 mg

PEANUT BUTTER AND JELLY CHIA PUDDING

Preparation Time: 10 min
Cooking Time: none
Mode of Cooking: No Cooking
Servings: 2
Ingredients:

- 1 cup unsweetened almond milk
- 3 Tbsp chia seeds
- 2 Tbsp peanut butter, unsweetened
- 1 Tbsp strawberry jam, sugar-free
- ½ tsp vanilla extract

Directions:

1. Blend almond milk, chia seeds, peanut butter, and vanilla extract in a bowl
2. Ensure the mixture is thoroughly mixed to distribute the peanut butter evenly
3. Let it rest overnight in the refrigerator
4. Before serving, top with sugar-free strawberry jam and additional peanut butter if desired

Tips:

- For a smoother texture, blend the peanut butter with a bit of almond milk before adding to the mixture
- Substitute any sugar-free jam to suit your taste preferences

Nutritional Values: Calories: 195, Fat: 11g, Carbs: 19g, Protein: 7g, Sugar: 4g, Sodium: 45 mg, Potassium: 150 mg, Cholesterol: 0 mg

3. REFRESHING BEVERAGES

LAVENDER LEMON BLISS TEA

Preparation Time: 10 min
Cooking Time: none
Mode of Cooking: Infusion
Servings: 4
Ingredients:

- 4 cups water
- 1 Tbsp dried lavender buds
- Peel of 1 lemon, avoiding the white pith
- 2 Tbsp honey
- Ice cubes for serving

Directions:

1. Heat water until just steaming, not boiling
2. Pour over lavender buds and lemon peel in a heat-proof pitcher
3. Cover and let steep for 5 to 7 min
4. Strain the infusion into a new pitcher and stir in honey until dissolved
5. Chill in the refrigerator until cold or serve over ice

Tips:

- Use fresh lemon peel for the best flavor and to avoid bitterness
- If preferred, garnish with fresh lavender sprigs to enhance the floral aroma

Nutritional Values: Calories: 50, Fat: 0g, Carbs: 13g, Protein: 0g, Sugar: 12g, Sodium: 0mg, Potassium: 3mg, Cholesterol: 0mg

MINTY GINGER GREEN TEA

Preparation Time: 15 min
Cooking Time: none
Mode of Cooking: Infusion
Servings: 4
Ingredients:

- 4 cups water
- 1 Tbsp green tea leaves
- 1 Tbsp fresh mint leaves
- 1 inch piece of ginger, thinly sliced
- 1 Tbsp honey
- Ice cubes for serving

Directions:

1. Heat water until just before boiling
2. Add green tea leaves, mint leaves, and ginger slices to a teapot
3. Pour hot water over the leaves and ginger
4. Let steep for about 10 min
5. Strain the tea into a pitcher
6. Stir in honey until dissolved
7. Refrigerate to cool or serve immediately over ice

Tips:

- Muddle the mint leaves lightly before adding them to the teapot to release more flavor
- For a stronger ginger taste, let the ginger slices steep for an additional 5 min

Nutritional Values: Calories: 25, Fat: 0g, Carbs: 6g, Protein: 0g, Sugar: 6g, Sodium: 0mg, Potassium: 9mg, Cholesterol: 0mg

CHAMOMILE APPLE ZEST TEA

Preparation Time: 12 min
Cooking Time: none
Mode of Cooking: Infusion
Servings: 4
Ingredients:

- 4 cups water
- 2 Tbsp dried chamomile flowers
- 1 apple, quartered and thinly sliced
- 1 cinnamon stick
- 2 Tbsp honey
- Ice cubes for serving

Directions:

1. Heat water to a near simmer
2. Place chamomile flowers, apple slices, and cinnamon stick in a large teapot
3. Pour the hot water over them
4. Let steep for 8 min
5. Remove cinnamon stick and strain the tea into a pitcher
6. Stir in honey while still warm
7. Chill in the refrigerator or serve over ice

Tips:

- Adding apple slices during the steeping process infuses a gentle, sweet flavor
- Use organic honey to keep the recipe natural and healthful

Nutritional Values: Calories: 60, Fat: 0g, Carbs: 15g, Protein: 0g, Sugar: 14g, Sodium: 0mg, Potassium: 32mg, Cholesterol: 0mg

TROPICAL MANGO BLISS SMOOTHIE

Preparation Time: 5 min.
Cooking Time: none
Mode of Cooking: Blending
Servings: 2
Ingredients:

- 1 ripe mango, peeled and cubed
- 1 banana, sliced
- 1/2 C. pineapple chunks
- 1/2 C. coconut water
- 1 Tbsp. flaxseeds
- 1/2 tsp. freshly grated ginger

Directions:

1. Combine all ingredients in a blender and blend until smooth
2. Pour into glasses and serve immediately

Tips:

- Use frozen fruit to make the smoothie cooler and thicker
- Add a scoop of protein powder for an extra boost of energy

Nutritional Values: Calories: 180, Fat: 2g, Carbs: 43g, Protein: 3g, Sugar: 35g, Sodium: 30mg, Potassium: 500mg, Cholesterol: 0mg

BERRY ANTIOXIDANT FUSION

Preparation Time: 10 min.
Cooking Time: none
Mode of Cooking: Blending
Servings: 2
Ingredients:

- 1 C. mixed berries (strawberries, blueberries, raspberries, blackberries), fresh or frozen
- 1 C. Greek yogurt, plain
- 1/2 C. almond milk
- 1 Tbsp. honey
- 1 Tbsp. chia seeds
- 4-5 mint leaves

Directions:

1. Combine berries, Greek yogurt, almond milk, honey, and chia seeds in a blender and blend until creamy
2. Add mint leaves for the last few seconds of blending for a fresh twist

3. Serve chilled

Tips:

- Freeze your berries ahead of time to make the smoothie extra refreshing
- Substitute honey with agave nectar if preferred

Nutritional Values: Calories: 220, Fat: 3g, Carbs: 40g, Protein: 8g, Sugar: 28g, Sodium: 55mg, Potassium: 332mg, Cholesterol: 10mg

GREEN GODDESS SMOOTHIE

Preparation Time: 8 min.
Cooking Time: none
Mode of Cooking: Blending
Servings: 1
Ingredients:

- 1 C. spinach leaves
- 1/2 ripe avocado, peeled and pitted
- 1/2 C. cucumber slices
- 1 kiwifruit, peeled and sliced
- 1 C. green tea (chilled)
- 1 Tbsp. lemon juice
- 1 tsp. spirulina powder

Directions:

1. Place all ingredients into a blender and blend until smooth and uniform
2. Pour into a large glass and enjoy immediately

Tips:

- Add a bit of ginger for an extra zing
- Spirulina powder can be substituted with wheatgrass powder for a different nutrient profile

Nutritional Values: Calories: 190, Fat: 8g, Carbs: 29g, Protein: 4g, Sugar: 12g, Sodium: 40mg, Potassium: 846mg, Cholesterol: 0mg

CLASSIC ZESTY LEMONADE

Preparation Time: 5 min
Cooking Time: none
Mode of Cooking: Mixing
Servings: 8
Ingredients:

- 4 cups water
- 1 cup fresh lemon juice (about 4-6 lemons)
- 1/3 cup honey or to taste
- 2 tsp freshly grated lemon zest
- Fresh mint leaves (optional) for garnish

Directions:

1. Combine lemon juice, honey, and half the water in a large pitcher and stir until honey is dissolved
2. Add the rest of the water and lemon zest, then stir again to mix well
3. Add ice cubes and mint leaves before serving

Tips:

- Adjust sweetness with more or less honey according to your taste
- Using cold water and serving immediately keeps it fresh and zesty

Nutritional Values: Calories: 50 per serving, Fat: 0g, Carbs: 14g, Protein: 0g, Sugar: 12g, Sodium: 2 mg, Potassium: 31 mg, Cholesterol: 0 mg

LAVENDER INFUSED LEMONADE

Preparation Time: 10 min
Cooking Time: none
Mode of Cooking: Infusing
Servings: 6
Ingredients:

- 5 cups water
- 1 cup fresh lemon juice
- 1/2 cup sugar
- 1 Tbsp dried lavender buds
- Ice cubes
- Lemon slices for garnish

Directions:

1. In a saucepan, combine 1 cup of water with sugar and lavender buds

2. Heat until sugar dissolves completely, then remove from heat and let sit for 5 minutes to infuse
3. Strain the lavender and mix the infused water with the remaining water and lemon juice in a pitcher
4. Chill and serve with ice cubes and lemon slices

Tips:

- For a richer lavender flavor, allow the buds to infuse for an additional 5 min
- Serve with a slice of lemon or a sprig of mint for enhanced flavor and presentation

Nutritional Values: Calories: 80 per serving, Fat: 0g, Carbs: 21g, Protein: 0g, Sugar: 20g, Sodium: 3 mg, Potassium: 31 mg, Cholesterol: 0 mg

SPARKLING GINGER LEMONADE

Preparation Time: 7 min
Cooking Time: none
Mode of Cooking: Mixing
Servings: 4

Ingredients:

- 3 cups chilled sparkling water
- 1 cup lemon juice
- 1/3 cup ginger syrup
- 1 lemon, thinly sliced for garnish
- Mint sprigs for garnish

Directions:

1. Mix lemon juice and ginger syrup in a pitcher
2. Add chilled sparkling water and stir gently to combine
3. Serve over ice and garnish with lemon slices and mint sprigs

Tips:

- Use a ginger-infused simple syrup for an extra kick
- The sparkling water should be added just before serving to maintain its fizz

Nutritional Values: Calories: 120 per serving, Fat: 0g, Carbs: 31g, Protein: 0g, Sugar: 29g, Sodium: 4 mg, Potassium: 49 mg, Cholesterol: 0 mg

CHAPTER 11: 4-WEEK MEAL PLAN

Embarking on a new dietary journey can often feel like navigating an unfamiliar city without a map. This section, however, is designed to be your trusted GPS through the landscapes of the DASH diet, ensuring that every turn you take leads to health and happiness. As we explore the next 4 weeks together, imagine each recipe as a scenic stop, and each tip as a shortcut, designed to make your travel through the new dietary changes straightforward and stress-free.

The beauty of a structured meal plan is much like crafting a well-oiled itinerary for a dream vacation. It eliminates the guesswork and the recurring question of "What's for dinner?" that can often lead to less-than-ideal meal decisions. Over the next 28 days, you will find yourself gradually building a solid foundation, ensuring that the DASH diet becomes as natural to you as your morning routine.

Week by week, you'll gain not just dishes to savor, but also confidence in your ability to maintain a balanced diet even on your busiest days. Each recipe is a building block in creating a resilient lifestyle that embraces nutritious, easy-to-prepare meals without sacrificing flavor or your precious time. This part of your journey is designed to reinforce the habits you've started to develop, providing you with everything you need to continue on the path of wellness.

By the end of these four weeks, you won't just have a collection of great recipes; you'll have woven the Dash diet into the fabric of your everyday life, equipped to make healthful food choices instinctively. Let this meal plan serve not only as your guide but also as your motivation to transform your diet into one of delicious, heart-healthy meals that cater to your hectic schedule and nourish both your body and soul. Here's to new beginnings and to a healthier, happier you!

TIPS FOR SUCCESS

Embarking on the four-week DASH diet meal plan is like starting a new adventure. It's thrilling and, admittedly, a bit daunting, but with the right mindset and practical strategies, you'll find yourself navigating it with the ease and confidence of an experienced traveler. Let us consider how preparing for your dietary journey can be as rewarding as achieving your healthy eating goals.

Imagine your first week on the DASH diet as setting out on a long-desired road trip. You've marked your map, planned your stops, and you're ready to go. But what makes a trip successful isn't just the route you take; it's also the preparations you make. One of the fundamental keys to success in your first week, and each week following, is planning. Take some time each weekend to look ahead. Which recipes are you looking forward to trying? What ingredients will you need? Planning your meals can turn what seems like a chore into an exciting part of your week—like choosing the next destination on your journey.

As you progress into the second week, you might begin to encounter the reality of daily life mixing with your new eating habits. Here, adaptability becomes your closest ally. Let's say you planned a scrumptious grilled vegetable platter for Thursday's dinner, but unexpected overtime at work means you're too tired to cook. This is where a quick yet nutritious alternative from your pre-prepared ingredients shines. Just like a savvy traveler might switch plans due to weather, having a backup plan ready ensures you stay on track without stress.

Approaching the third and fourth weeks, your initial enthusiasm may begin to wane—as it does with any long-term venture. This is a perfect moment to remind yourself of the 'why' behind your journey. Remember, every nutritious meal is a step toward better health and well-being. To rekindle your enthusiasm, you might introduce a little variety or tweak recipes to rediscover the excitement. Think of it as adding an impromptu detour to your journey to explore an uncharted attraction.

Throughout the weeks, there's also the aspect of community. Just as travelers share tales and tips, don't overlook the value of sharing your journey. Engage with friends or online communities who are also adopting the DASH diet. Sharing experiences can offer new insights or motivate you to keep going when the going gets tough.

Moreover, be gentle with yourself. If you stray off path momentarily, don't view it as a failure but as part of the learning curve—essential and inevitable. Each day presents a new opportunity to steer back. It's similar to missing a turn and finding a new little cafe that becomes your go-to spot. These little 'mistakes' can fortify your resolve and enhance your experience.

Lastly, celebrate your milestones, no matter how small. Did you follow through with planned meals all week? That's fantastic! Or perhaps you found a way to increase your vegetable intake. Celebrate these wins. Rewards build motivation, and motivation fuels further success. Each small victory is a building block towards a healthier you.

By the end of your four-week meal plan challenge, these practices won't just be strategies; they'll be part of your new lifestyle. Think back to how the journey began, full of uncertainties and excitement, and look at you now—more knowledgeable and confident. As you continue on your wellness path with the DASH diet, remember, it's not just about following a set of rules. It's about creating a vibrant, healthful life that lasts well beyond these initial weeks. Here's to enjoying the journey, every step of the way!

ADJUSTMENTS AND VARIATIONS

Imagine you're four weeks deep into your DASH journey with our carefully crafted meal plan, and things are going splendidly. You're feeling healthier, your family is enjoying the meals, and then, as life always does, it throws you a curveball. A sudden business trip, a family function, or perhaps the grocery store is out of a key ingredient you need for tonight's dinner. This is where the beauty of adjustments and variations comes into its own.

The DASH diet, with its rich variety and flexibility, allows for such adjustments without throwing your goals off track. Let's talk about how you can navigate these situations and continue to enjoy your Dash diet meals without stress.

Firstly, the secret lies in the art of substitution. Suppose your planned meal calls for quinoa, and you only have brown rice on hand. Both grains are excellent sources of nutrients and fit well within the DASH diet's guidelines. Use the rice! The goal is to maintain a balanced diet, not to stick rigidly to specific ingredients. The same goes for vegetables and proteins. No spinach? Try kale! No chicken breast available? Go for turkey or even a plant-based alternative if you're feeling adventurous.

Next, consider the portion control aspect of the DASH diet, which is crucial in managing blood pressure and overall health. If you're faced with a meal choice that seems daunting, focus on portion sizes. You can often make a less-than-ideal meal fit your diet better by adjusting how much of it you eat. Pair it with a salad or a serving of steamed vegetables to fill you up without overdoing it on sodium or calories.

Sometimes, you might find yourself at a restaurant or a family gathering where the DUMB options are limited. This is a great chance to practice the skill of plate balancing. Fill half your plate with vegetables, a quarter with lean protein, and the rest with a whole grain or another complex carb. This method ensures you're hitting all your nutritional markers, even if the dish isn't strictly a DASH recipe.

Remember, the DASH diet isn't just about following a strict set of rules—it's about learning to make healthier choices in any situation. It's fine to adapt the diet to your personal preferences and life circumstances. Suppose you are a vegetarian or someone in your family is allergic to nuts; these individual needs can also guide your adjustments. The DASH diet is versatile enough to accommodate these without compromising on flavor or nutrition.

Lastly, it's important to keep the conversation going. Whether it's talking with family members about your diet needs to prepare them for change or discussing your meal plan with a dietitian for personalized advice, communication plays a key role in the success of your diet. Never hesitate to discuss your concerns or seek guidance when new situations arise.

Adjustments and variations are not just a response to unforeseen circumstances but an integral part of embracing a healthy, flexible eating lifestyle. Each challenge offers a chance to become more adept at managing your diet and, ultimately, your health. So, take each little hiccup as an opportunity to learn and grow in your DASH diet journey.

LONG-TERM TIPS AND STRATEGIES

As you embark on your journey with the DASH diet through our 4-week meal plan, you'll discover not just a plethora of delicious recipes but also a blueprint for a sustainable way of eating that can transform your health. But what happens after these four weeks? The true challenge, and the real magic, lies in seamlessly integrating these new eating habits into your daily routine long-term.

Imagine this: You've followed the meal plans, felt the benefits—perhaps you've even noticed that your blood dynamics have improved, or you've got more energy throughout the day. Now, it's about maintaining that momentum in a way that feels as natural as your morning coffee.

One of the most effective strategies is to slowly but confidently become your own meal planner. Start with familiar recipes from the meal plan you enjoyed, and begin experimenting with similar ingredients or cooking methods. For instance, if the Avocado and Bean Salad captured your heart, think about swapping out black beans for chickpeas or adding some spiced baked tofu for extra protein. These subtle shifts will not only introduce variety but also keep your tastebuds intrigued.

Another key to long-term success is setting a routine that aligns with your lifestyle. Were Sunday afternoons perfect for prepping meals in advance? Or did you find quick 15-minute recipes that fit better with your bustling weekdays? Recognize these patterns and craft your cooking schedule around them. It feels less like an added chore and more like a natural part of your week.

Now, let's talk grocery shopping—a critical aspect that can be both a pleasure and a challenge. Post the initial 4-week plan, you'll likely have a better grasp on reading food labels and identifying what's best for your DASH diet. Use this newfound knowledge to venture out from the usual grocery list. Explore local markets for fresh produce, or try online stores for bulk ingredients that save time and money. It becomes a culinary adventure rather than a daunting task.

Eating out can also align with your DASH goals. When dining with friends or family, look for restaurants with heart-healthy choices. Don't hesitate to ask for dressings or sauces on the side and opt for steamed, grilled, or broiled dishes instead of those that are fried or creamy. This way, you're still in tune with your health goals, without feeling restricted.

Lastly, integrating the DASH diet into your family life can be a joyful journey. Involve your partner or kids in meal planning and cooking. Their involvement not only eases the load but also helps everyone understand and appreciate the benefits of healthy eating habits. When the family looks forward to a nutritious dinner, it becomes more than just a meal; it becomes a cherished part of the day.

Building a sustainable, healthy eating pattern doesn't happen overnight, but the DASH diet is designed to be flexible and adaptable. It's about finding joy in the kitchen, making peace with your plate, and being kind to your body. With these strategies in your back pocket, you're not just following a diet; you're embracing a vibrant, healthier lifestyle that lasts. Keep this spirit alive, and watch how simple, wholesome eating can become your second nature. It's not just about the food on your plate but about creating a lifestyle that sustains your vitality and wellness — effortlessly.

1. Week 1: Getting Started

WEEK 1	breakfast	snack	lunch	snack	dinner
Monday	Classic Berry Almond Overnight Oats	Spiced Maple Cinnamon Nut Mix	Mediterranean Chickpea Salad with Sun-Dried Tomatoes	Snap Pea Crisps with Curry Yogurt Dip	Herbed Citrus Salmon with Fennel
Tuesday	Peanut Butter Banana Overnight Oats	Apple Slices with Almond-Cinnamon Butter	Classic Grilled Chicken Wraps	Garlic Parmesan Roasted Chickpeas	Mediterranean Quinoa Stuffed Bell Peppers
Wednesday	Tropical Coconut Overnight Oats	Banana Medallions with Peanut Butter and Flaxseeds	Smoky Lentil and Spinach Soup	Zesty Bell Pepper Sticks with Avocado Lime Hummus	Garlic Mushroom and Spinach Quinoa
Thursday	Berry Almond Sunrise Bowl	Sesame Seed & Chia Energy Bites	Greek Chickpea Salad with Herbed Yogurt Dressing	Herbed Goat Cheese Stuffed Cherry Tomatoes	Spicy Grilled Chicken with Bell Pepper Salsa
Friday	Green Tropical Energy Bowl	Pistachio & Cranberry Salt-free Trail Mix	Mediterranean Turkey Wrap	Tropical Cottage Cheese Delight	Lemon Herb Grilled Chicken with Asparagus
Saturday	Peanut Butter Banana Bliss Bowl	Almond Coconut Energy Bars	Quinoa & Turkey Stuffed Bell Peppers	Honey Cinnamon Roasted Chickpeas	Sundried Tomato and Garlic Chicken Stew
Sunday	Cinnamon Spice Whole Grain Pancakes	Pistachio and Date Breakfast Bars	Whole Wheat Pasta Primavera with Spring Vegetables	Classic Carrot and Cucumber Sticks with Spiced Hummus	Coconut Curry Chicken Stew

Grains and Baking
- Oats
- Whole grain flour
- Whole wheat wrap
- Whole wheat pasta
- Quinoa

Dairy and Alternatives
- Almond milk
- Greek yogurt
- Milk
- Cottage cheese
- Feta cheese
- Goat cheese

Protein
- Chicken breast
- Turkey breast
- Salmon
- Lentils
- Chickpeas

Fruits
- Berries
- Banana
- Pineapple
- Apple
- Lemon
- Lime

Vegetables
- Spinach
- Lettuce
- Tomato
- Avocado
- Bell peppers
- Zucchini
- Carrot
- Peas
- Cucumber
- Onion
- Garlic
- Mushrooms
- Asparagus
- Fennel
- Snap peas
- Cherry tomatoes

Nuts and Seeds
- Almonds
- Mixed nuts
- Sesame seeds
- Chia seeds
- Pistachios
- Flaxseeds
- Dates

Condiments and Spices
- Honey
- Maple syrup
- Cinnamon
- Smoked paprika
- Curry powder
- Olive oil
- Lemon juice
- Herbs (dill, cilantro)
- Baking powder

Other
- Almond butter
- Peanut butter
- Hummus
- Tomato sauce
- Chicken broth

2. Week 2: Building Momentum

WEEK 2	breakfast	snack	lunch	snack	dinner
Monday	Spinach and Mushroom Frittata	Pomegranate and Pistachio Greek Yogurt Parfait	Avocado and Chickpea Salad with Pomegranate	Almond Coconut Energy Bars	Maple-Glazed Salmon with Sage
Tuesday	Bell Pepper and Potato Frittata	Tropical Coconut Greek Yogurt Parfait	Citrus Kissed Quinoa and Black Bean Salad	Creamy Spinach and Artichoke Dip	Mediterranean Grilled Chicken and Veggie Kabobs
Wednesday	Asparagus and Goat Cheese Frittata	Chia and Pumpkin Seed Power Bars	Tropical Spinach and Strawberry Salad	Mini Caprese Skewers	Pistachio Crusted Salmon
Thursday	Spicy Avocado Toast with Egg	Turkey and Spinach Muffin Tin Omelets	Classic Turkey and Avocado Sandwich	Spiced Maple Cinnamon Nut Mix	Lemon Herb Grilled Chicken with Asparagus
Friday	Mediterranean Avocado Toast	Mushroom and Swiss Muffin Tin Omelets	Spicy Thai Chicken Wraps	Apple Slices with Almond-Cinnamon Butter	Garlic Mushroom and Spinach Quinoa
Saturday	Smoked Salmon Avocado Toast	Spinach and Feta Muffin Tin Omelets	Mediterranean Veggie Hummus Pita	Banana Medallions with Peanut Butter and Flaxseeds	Spicy Grilled Chicken with Bell Pepper Salsa
Sunday	Sunrise Berry & Granola Greek Yogurt Parfait	Pistachio & Cranberry Salt-free Trail Mix	Roasted Bell Pepper and Hummus Pita	Sesame Seed & Chia Energy Bites	Quinoa & Turkey Stuffed Bell Peppers

Grains and Baking
- Oats
- Whole grain bread
- Whole wheat wrap
- Pita bread

Dairy and Alternatives
- Milk
- Cheese
- Goat cheese
- Feta cheese
- Greek yogurt
- Swiss cheese
- Mozzarella

Protein
- Chicken breast
- Turkey
- Smoked salmon
- Salmon

Fruits
- Berries
- Banana
- Pineapple
- Apple
- Lemon
- Lime
- Pomegranate seeds
- Citrus fruits
- Strawberries

Vegetables
- Spinach
- Mushrooms
- Bell peppers
- Potatoes
- Asparagus
- Tomato
- Lettuce
- Carrot
- Cucumber
- Zucchini
- Artichokes
- Cherry tomatoes
- Basil
- Onion
- Garlic

Nuts and Seeds
- Almonds
- Mixed nuts
- Pistachios
- Chia seeds
- Pumpkin seeds
- Sesame seeds
- Flaxseeds

Condiments and Spices
- Honey
- Maple syrup
- Cinnamon
- Red pepper flakes
- Olive oil
- Peanut sauce
- Herbs (dill, cilantro)
- Tomato sauce

Other
- Almond butter
- Peanut butter
- Hummus
- Dates

3. WEEK 3 & 4: SUSTAINING THE DASH LIFESTYLE

WEEK 3	breakfast	snack	lunch	snack	dinner
Monday	Spinach and Feta Breakfast Burritos	Spinach and Feta Muffin Tin Omelets	Mediterranean Chickpea Salad with Sun-Dried Tomatoes	Creamy Spinach and Artichoke Dip	Mediterranean Quinoa Stuffed Bell Peppers
Tuesday	Turkey and Avocado Ranch Burritos	Mushroom and Swiss Muffin Tin Omelets	Avocado and Chickpea Salad with Pomegranate	Mini Caprese Skewers	Curried Coconut Quinoa with Lentils
Wednesday	Mushroom and Bell Pepper Breakfast Burritos	Turkey and Spinach Muffin Tin Omelets	Greek Chickpea Salad with Herbed Yogurt Dressing	Spiced Maple Cinnamon Nut Mix	Garlic Mushroom and Spinach Quinoa
Thursday	Cinnamon Spice Whole Grain Pancakes	Chia and Pumpkin Seed Power Bars	Citrus Kissed Quinoa and Black Bean Salad	Apple Slices with Almond-Cinnamon Butter	Sundried Tomato and Garlic Chicken Stew
Friday	Blueberry Lemon Whole Grain Pancakes	Almond Coconut Energy Bars	Mediterranean Quinoa and Black Bean Salad	Banana Medallions with Peanut Butter and Flaxseeds	Coconut Curry Chicken Stew
Saturday	Apple Cinnamon Oatmeal Pancakes	Pistachio and Date Breakfast Bars	Tropical Quinoa and Black Bean Salad	Sesame Seed & Chia Energy Bites	Mushroom and Barley Chicken Stew
Sunday	Berry Almond Sunrise Bowl	Pistachio & Cranberry Salt-free Trail Mix	Tropical Spinach and Strawberry Salad	Pistachio & Cranberry Salt-free Trail Mix	Mediterranean Bliss Baked Cod

Grains and Baking
- Whole wheat tortillas
- Whole grain flour
- Baking powder
- Oats
- Barley

Dairy and Alternatives
- Milk
- Cheese
- Feta cheese
- Greek yogurt
- Swiss cheese
- Mozzarella

Protein
- Chicken breast
- Turkey
- Cod

Fruits
- Berries
- Apple
- Lemon
- Lime

- Pomegranate seeds
- Citrus fruits
- Strawberries
- Mango
- Banana

Vegetables
- Spinach
- Mushrooms
- Bell peppers
- Potatoes
- Asparagus
- Tomato
- Lettuce
- Carrot
- Cucumber
- Zucchini
- Artichokes
- Cherry tomatoes
- Basil
- Onion
- Garlic

Nuts and Seeds

- Almonds
- Mixed nuts
- Pistachios
- Chia seeds
- Pumpkin seeds
- Sesame seeds
- Flaxseeds

Condiments and Spices
- Honey
- Maple syrup
- Cinnamon
- Red pepper flakes
- Olive oil
- Peanut sauce
- Herbs (dill, cilantro)
- Tomato sauce

Other
- Almond butter
- Peanut butter
- Hummus
- Dates

WEEK 4	breakfast	snack	lunch	snack	dinner
Monday	Tropical Coconut Greek Yogurt Parfait	Minty Orange Peel Dark Chocolate Bark	Smoky Lentil and Spinach Soup	Lavender Lemon Bliss Tea	Herb-Infused Cod and Asparagus
Tuesday	Pomegranate and Pistachio Greek Yogurt Parfait	Rosemary Hazelnut Dark Chocolate Bark	Moroccan Lentil and Veggie Stew	Minty Ginger Green Tea	Mediterranean Bliss Baked Cod
Wednesday	Kiwi Lime Greek Yogurt Parfait	Cherry Pistachio Dark Chocolate Bark	Italian Lentil and Tomato Soup	Chamomile Apple Zest Tea	Spiced Orange Cod Delight
Thursday	Grilled Peaches with Honey and Thyme	Classic Low-Sodium Oatmeal Raisin Cookies	Creamy Tomato Basil Soup with Greek Yogurt	Tropical Mango Bliss Smoothie	Cinnamon Spice Baked Apples
Friday	Grilled Peach and Ricotta Crostini	Almond Oatmeal Cookies with Date Purée	Smoky Roasted Tomato Soup	Berry Antioxidant Fusion	Maple Ginger Baked Apples
Saturday	Peaches Grilled with Vanilla and Ginger	Oatmeal Spice Cookies	Spicy Tomato and Red Lentil Soup	Green Goddess Smoothie	Almond Crunch Baked Apples
Sunday	Classic Vanilla Chia Seed Pudding	Classic Zesty Lemonade	Classic Turkey and Avocado Sandwich	Cottage Cheese Pineapple Rings	Mixed Berry and Chia Parfait

Grains and Baking
- Barley
- Whole wheat pasta
- Whole wheat flour
- Baking powder
- Oatmeal
- Wild rice

Dairy and Alternatives
- Parmesan cheese
- Feta cheese
- Almond milk
- Greek yogurt
- Cream

Protein
- Chicken breast
- Cod
- Turkey

Fruits
- Avocado
- Lemon
- Lime
- Orange
- Mango
- Mixed berries
- Banana
- Apples
- Pomegranate seeds

Vegetables
- Mushrooms
- Onion
- Garlic
- Spring vegetables
- Tomatoes
- Olives
- Edamame
- Asparagus
- Lettuce
- Tomato
- Spinach

Nuts and Seeds
- Cashews
- Pistachios
- Almonds
- Chia seeds

Condiments and Spices
- Olive oil
- Sesame oil
- Soy sauce
- Red pepper flakes
- Spices
- Vanilla extract
- Honey
- Maple syrup
- Cinnamon
- Mint extract
- Rosemary
- Lavender

Other
- Dark chocolate
- Dates
- Vegetable broth
- Chicken broth
- Whole grain bread
- Sparkling water
- Mint
- Ginger
- Green tea
- Chamomile
- Apple zest

Made in the USA
Monee, IL
23 February 2025